Science NG
Student Guide

K12 Summit
CURRICULUM

About K12 Inc.
K12 Inc. (NYSE: LRN) drives innovation and advances the quality of education by delivering state-of-the-art digital learning platforms and technology to students and school districts around the world. K12 is a company of educators offering its online and blended curriculum to charter schools, public school districts, private schools, and directly to families. More information can be found at K12.com.

978-1-60153-597-9

Printed by Bradford & Bigelow, Newburyport, MA, USA, September 2020

Table of Contents

Student Guide
Populations

On our wonderful planet, nature tries to keep everything in balance. Plants and animals live in close communities as they pass through the cycle of birth and death. They compete for food, water, and shelter in a never-ending dance that creates the complex web we call life on Earth.

A school of fish, a herd of cows, and a stand of maple trees—what do they have in common? All are groups of individuals of the same type that live together, or a *population*. Explore how members of a population are distributed within the area in which they live, and find out how the size of a population may change over time.

Lesson Objectives

- Calculate a change in population size.
- Define *sampling* as a way to estimate the size and distribution of a population.
- Identify birth and immigration as the two main factors that cause an increase in a population.
- Identify death and emigration as the two main factors that cause a decrease in a population.
- Identify individuals in a population as clumped, uniformly spaced, or randomly spaced.
- State that a *population* is a group of individuals of the same type living in a certain area.
- Identify the resource, such as food, sunlight, water, and space, for which organisms are competing.

PREPARE

Approximate lesson time is 60 minutes.

Materials

For the Student

> Sample the Space
> household item - shoe box lid
> pencil
> rice, uncooked
> ruler
> scissors
> Sample Your Own Space
> field guide
> sticks (4)
> magnifying glass
> paper, 8 1/2" x 11"
> string

Keywords and Pronunciation

emigration: Movement or migration out of a population. The ducks left the area when the lake dried up, and they emigrated to a lake in the next county.

immigration: Movement or migration into a population. Foxes immigrated into the national park and stayed there among the resident foxes.

migration: A regular movement of animals to a different location because of weather conditions, or of food, water, or shelter requirements. Many birds in northern lands migrate south in the winter to escape the cold weather.

population: A group of individuals of the same type that live in a certain area at a certain time. The population of deer grew larger every year after the wolves left the area.

sampling: The process of observing or counting a small part of a population as an indicator of the whole. Scientists may take a sampling of organisms to study its distribution.

LEARN

Activity 1: Changing Populations *(Online)*

Activity 2: Sample the Space *(Offline)*

How do ecologists figure out how many individuals are in a population? Try a sampling method used by ecologists in the field.

ASSESS

Lesson Assessment: Populations *(Online)*

You will complete an online assessment covering the main objectives of this lesson.

LEARN

Activity 3: Optional: Sample Your Own Space *(Offline)*

What organisms live where you live? Become a scientist and sample your own environment.

Name _____ Date _____

Populations

Sample the Space

Practice sampling a population to figure out how many individuals are in an area.

1. Use a ruler to draw a grid of 12 equal squares on the inside of a shoe box lid.

2. Pour in about 1 tablespoon of rice. Shake the box gently to spread out the rice.

3. Choose one square as your sample plot. Count the grains of rice in that square, and write the number on the box lid, inside the square.

4. Multiply the amount of rice in the square by 12. Write that number in the list below next to the label "1 square sample."

5. You now have an estimate of the amount of rice in the box. You did not have to count all of the rice to find a good estimate. What would happen if you made your sample bigger? Complete the following steps to find out.

6. Choose 2 squares and count the rice inside. Multiply that number by 6. Write that number in the list.

7. Choose 3 squares, count the rice, and multiply by 4. Write that number in the list.

8. Choose 6 squares, count the rice, then multiply by 2. Write that number in the list.

9. Now count ALL of the rice grains. Write that number in the last space in the list.

List of Samples

- 1 square sample = _____
- 2 square sample = _____
- 3 square sample = _____
- 6 square sample = _____
- Total amount of rice = _____

Which sample gave you the better estimate?

_____

Sampling allows you to study a population without studying the whole population. A larger sample will give closer estimates, but at some point, your estimates will not get much better, no matter how many samples you study.

Name _____   Date _____

Populations
Sample Your Own Space

You'll never know what's living in your own ecosystem if you don't get down on your hands and knees and explore. By observing a small sample of your environment, you can get a good idea about the plant and animal interactions going on there. After completing the steps below, make sketches and answer the questions to conduct a detailed study of your site.

- Find a convenient area (the grassier the better).
- Measure out a square that is 1 meter all around. Place sticks at each corner of the square.
- Tie string to the sticks to make the square.

1. First observe the plant life in your site. Make sketches and write down detailed descriptions. Use a field guide to find out names of the plants you find. If you can't find the name, make one up.

2. How many different types of plants did you find?

_____

3. Which is the smallest plant? The biggest?

_____

_____

4. Which plant did you find the most of? The least?

_____

_____

5. What do the plants you found have in common?

_____

_____

6. Next observe the animal life in your site. Make sketches and describe any animals you see.

7. How many different types of animals did you find?

_____

8. Did you hear animal's sounds but not see any animals?

_____

9. Did you see evidence of animals, but not see the animals themselves?

_____

10. Which is the biggest animal you found? The smallest?

_____

_____

11. Which animal did you find the most of? The least?

_____

_____

12. How does the plant life affect the animals in your sample?

_____

_____

_____

13. How does the animal life affect the plant life in your sample?

_____

_____

_____

Student Guide

Competition

How do different living things in a community use limited amounts of water, space, and food? Look at the relationships between organisms as they compete for resources within the same area.

Lesson Objectives

- Identify the resource, such as food, sunlight, water, and space, for which organisms are competing.
- Name two ways animals avoid, or reduce, competition (for example, moving to other habitats, eating different types of food, hunting at different times).
- Recognize that competition can occur among individuals of the same species in the same population as well as among different species in different populations.
- Recognize ways in which organisms in a community compete for food, water, and space.
- Recognize that in predator-prey relationships, the size of each population can change in regular cycles.

PREPARE

Approximate lesson time is 60 minutes.

Materials

For the Student

Hare-y Competition

Keywords and Pronunciation

Galápagos (guh-LAH-puh-guhs)

competition: The struggle between two or more organisms or two or more kinds of organisms for resources in short supply. Lions in the same population are in competition with each other for food resources.

resource: Materials from the environment that living things use to live and grow. Food, water, and shelter are resources animals need to survive.

LEARN

Activity 1: Competition *(Online)*

Activity 2: Hare-y Competition *(Online)*

Play a game to observe the results of competition for food, water, and shelter among a population of hares.

ASSESS

Lesson Assessment: Competition *(Offline)*

You will complete an offline assessment covering the main objectives of this lesson. Your learning coach will score this assessment.

Name _____ Date _____

Competition

Hare-y Competition

Animals cannot live without food, water, and space or shelter. Animals compete with one another for these resources. Changes in the availability of resources cause changes in animal populations. If plenty of food, water, and shelter are available, animals survive and reproduce, and the population increases. If not enough food, water, and shelter are available, some animals die or move away, and the population decreases. Sometimes there will be no water available due to a drought. There may be a food shortage or no shelter because of habitat destruction.

The Hare-y Competition activity is a simulation. A *simulation* acts out a process. This simulation acts out a *competition*.

As you observe the competition among the hares, use the chart to record the number of hares that survive each year. Then transfer the hare population data from your chart to the bar graph and use the bar graph to answer the questions.

Year	1	2	3	4	5	6
Number of hares that survive						

Years

What do you notice about the hare population?

_____

_____

How can you tell when competition among hares was greatest? What happened next?

_____

_____

If you continued to track the hare population for 6 more years, do you think you would get a different population graph? Why or why not?

_____

_____

_____

_____

_____

Student Guide
Predators and Prey

Have you ever seen a film of a lion hunting down a zebra? Have you ever watched a cat chase a mouse? These are both examples of predator-prey relationships in different ecosystems. Learn how predator-prey relationships can affect population sizes.

Lesson Objectives

- Recognize that predator-prey relationships can help balance the structure of the community.
- Identify ways predators locate and capture their prey.
- Identify ways prey defend themselves against predators.
- Recognize that in predator-prey relationships, the size of each population can change in regular cycles.

PREPARE

Approximate lesson time is 60 minutes.

Materials

For the Student

> The Graph Tells It All
> pencil

Keywords and Pronunciation

herbivore (UR-buh-vor)**:** An animal that feeds mainly on plants. A cow is considered an herbivore since its diet is mainly plants.

predator: An animal that hunts for food. A hawk is a predator of mice.

prey: An animal or plant that is hunted for food. Berries and birds are both prey for the desert coyote.

LEARN

Activity 1: Predators and Prey *(Online)*

Activity 2: The Graph Tells It All *(Offline)*

Predator-prey populations can change in regular cycles. Scientists use graphs to show the rise and fall of populations and to point out some interesting relationships.

ASSESS

Lesson Assessment: Predators and Prey *(Offline)*

You will complete an offline assessment covering the main objectives of this lesson. Your learning coach will score this assessment.

Name _____   Date _____

Predators and Prey
The Graph Tells It All

Population Graphs

Graphs can show changes in population.

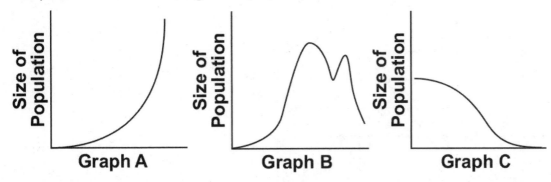

1. Which graph shows a population that rises and falls over time? _____

2. Which graph shows a population that has fallen to zero? _____

3. Study Graph C. What factors may have caused the population to decrease in this way?

_____

_____

_____

Deer Population Changes

This graph shows changes in a population of deer in Arizona between 1890 and 1930. These deer lived in a canyon along with mountain lions, which prey on deer. Notice how the deer population rises and falls.

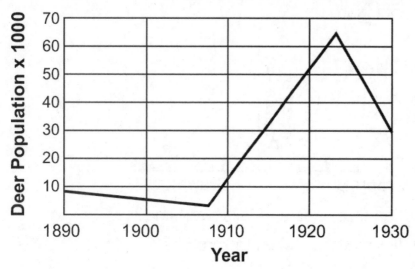

1. Can you tell what year people began killing mountain lions? Look for a sharp increase in the deer population. Why would the deer population increase?

   _____

   _____

   _____

   _____

2. Find where the deer population was highest. With so many deer competing for resources, what happened next?

   _____

   _____

   _____

   _____

The Lynx and the Hare

You can use graphs to study more than one population at a time. For example, about every 7 years, the snowshoe hare population rises, then crashes. Canada lynx population does the same thing, a year behind the hares. Look at this graph of the lynx and hare population.

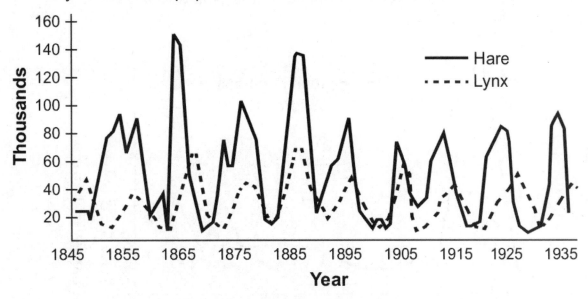

1. What happens after the hare population falls?

   _____

   _____

2. Which is the predator, the lynx or the hare? _____

3. How do you know which organisms are the predators and which are the prey?

   _____

   _____

   _____

   _____

   _____

The Wolf and the Moose

The wolf is a predator of the moose. A moose is very strong, so wolves usually will attack only moose that are old, sick, or young. At one time, a small herd of Canadian moose walked across a frozen lake to Isle Royale, an island in North America. There was a large supply of food for the moose. Soon, wolves reached the same island. This graph shows the changes in the wolf and moose population on the island.

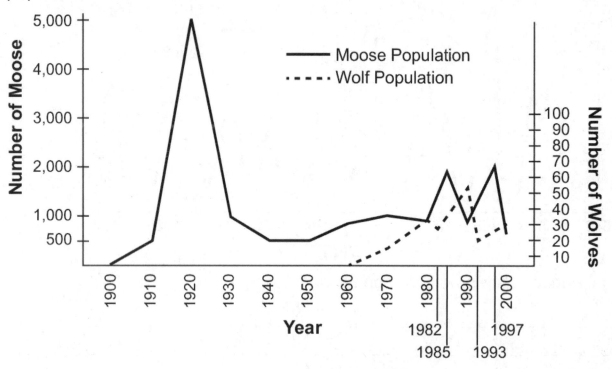

1. During what year was the moose population largest? _____

2. By 1928, the moose had eaten most of the plants they liked to eat. What happened next?

   _____

   _____

3. Study the wolf population. In 1980, many wolves became sick with a virus. What happened to the moose population?

   _____

   _____

4. What happened when the moose population grew too large again?

   _____

   _____

The Arctic Fox and the Lemming

In Canada live the arctic fox and the lemming—a small rodent. The arctic fox is an excellent swimmer. Its bark sounds like a small dog. Lemmings are herbivores. They usually live in colonies and are found near the water.

Scientists spent 15 years collecting the information in the graph below. Use this information to make your own graph on the next page that shows the relationship between the arctic fox and lemming population.

Year	Population of lemmings (in hundreds)	Population of arctic fox (in hundreds)
1	20	10
2	55	15
3	65	55
4	95	60
5	55	50
6	5	45
7	15	10
8	50	40
9	75	25
10	20	10
11	25	5
12	50	25
13	70	40
14	30	25
15	15	5

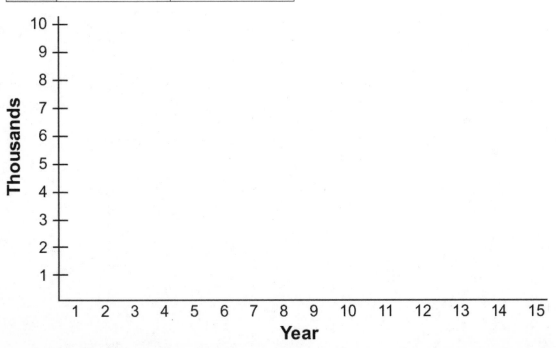

1. Which is the predator and which is the prey?

_____

2. How can you tell from the graph?

_____

_____

_____

_____

_____

_____

_____

Student Guide

Symbiosis

Leeches and ticks and barnacles, oh my! Learn how these and other creatures relate to other organisms in something called a *symbiotic relationship*. In *symbiosis,* two different kinds of organisms interact with each other and at least one of them benefits from the relationship.

Lesson Objectives

- Define *commensalism* as an interaction between two organisms in which one organism gains from the relationship and the neither benefits nor harms the other.
- Define *mutualism* as an interaction between two organisms in which both benefit from the relationship.
- Define *parasitism* as an interaction between two organisms in which one gains from the relationship and harms the other.
- Explain that the annual flooding of rivers allowed people to grow grain such as rice.
- Recognize that organisms in an ecosystem can compete for resources such as food, shelter, and water.
- Identify symbiotic relationships between organisms (mutualism, commensalism, and parasitism).

PREPARE

Approximate lesson time is 60 minutes.

Materials

For the Student

Relationship Studies
pencil

Keywords and Pronunciation

acacia (uh-KAY-shuh)

commensalism (kuh-MEN-suh-lih-zuhm): A symbiotic relationship in which one organism benefits and the other neither benefits nor is harmed. Barnacles attached to a whale is an example of commensalism.

mutualism (MYOO-chuh-wuh-lih-zuhm): A symbiotic relationship in which both types of organism help each other and both benefit. Bees pollinating flowers as they sip the flowers´nectar is an example of mutualism.

parasitism (PAIR-uh-suh-tih-zuhm): A symbiotic relationship in which one organism benefits and the other is harmed. A leech attaching to a host´s body and sucking the host´s blood is an example of parasitism.

symbiosis (sim-biy-OH-sis): A relationship between two organisms that interact in a way that benefits at least one of them. A tick and a dog live in symbiosis.

LEARN

Activity 1: Helpful and Harmful Relationships *(Online)*

Activity 2: Relationship Studies *(Offline)*

Identify the types of symbiotic relationships between organisms as mutualism, commensalism, or parasitism.

ASSESS

Lesson Assessment: Symbiosis *(Online)*

You will complete an online assessment covering the main objectives of this lesson.

Name _____ Date _____

Symbiosis

Relationship Studies

Plants and animals may have one of three types of relationships:

- Mutualism - Two organisms gain from the relationship.
- Commensalism - One organism gains from the relationship and the other neither benefits nor is harmed.
- Parasitism - One organism gains from the relationship while harming the other.

Read about the organisms below and tell what kind of relationship they have.

1. Snails make shells, then leave the shells. Hermit crabs find homes inside the empty snail shells. The snail is not harmed.

   _____

2. A honey guide bird shows a honey badger the way to beehive. The badger breaks open the hive and eats honey. The bird also eats the honey.

   _____

3. Mistletoe grows on an oak tree. The oak tree loses water and nutrients to the mistletoe.

   _____

4. Insects stick to a buffalo's hair as it walks through the grass. A cowbird eats the insects and does not harm the buffalo.

   _____

5. Ticks feed on a rhinoceros's blood.

   _____

6. Oxpeckers eat ticks on a rhinoceros.

   _____

7. Yucca moths lay eggs in yucca flowers. When the eggs hatch, the larvae eat the yucca seeds. The adult moths pollinate the flowers.

   _____

8. Bacteria live in your intestines. They make vitamin K, which is good for your blood. They also help digest food.

   _____

9. A different type of bacteria enters your body when you eat bad food or water. It causes you to lose fluids your body needs.

   _____

10. Sea anemones have stinging tentacles. A clownfish lives among the sea anemones without being stung. The clownfish helps clean the sea anemones.

   _____

Student Guide

Animal Behavior

Do animals learn behaviors from their parents? Or are they born just "knowing" what to do? Explore the behaviors of animals to find out why animals respond to the world in certain ways, as well as why some live and work together in social groups.

Lesson Objectives

- Identify behaviors as innate or learned.
- Classify organisms as predators and prey.
- Describe factors that affect the growth of a population.
- Explain that an animal's behavior helps it survive.
- Explain that living things cause changes in their ecosystems, and that some of these changes are detrimental to other organisms, and some are beneficial.
- Identify behaviors that help animals survive.
- Identify symbiotic relationships between organisms (mutualism, commensalism, and parasitism).
- Recognize that members of a society have special roles and work together to increase the group's chances of survival.
- Recognize that organisms in an ecosystem can compete for resources such as food, shelter, and water.
- State that a *population* is a group of individuals of the same type living in a certain area.

PREPARE

Approximate lesson time is 60 minutes.

Advance Preparation

- If you choose to do this alternate activity, you will need at least 10 live pill bugs (isopods). You can find them living under logs, moist leaves, flowerpots, outdoor pet dishes, or under paving bricks or stones. You may also purchase them from Carolina Biological at carolina.com. Allow a couple of weeks for delivery.

Materials

For the Student

Pill Bug Behaviors
pencil
Alternate Activity: Pill Bug Behaviors
household item - aluminum foil
household item - bowl (2)
household item - dish
household item - ice cubes
pill bugs
markers - black permanent
water - warm
paper, 8 1/2" x 11"

Keywords and Pronunciation

behavior: The way in which an organism responds to its environment. Behaviors may be learned or innate.

imprinting: Developing behaviors during a specific period of time. Imprinting usually occurs right after an organism is born.

innate: A type of behavior that is "built in" or does not have to be learned. Moving away from light is an innate behavior of pill bugs.

social behavior: Any interaction between organisms of the same kind. Male mountain goats fighting to defend their territory is a social behavior.

societies: Groups in which organisms live. Bees are an example of organisms that live in societies.

stimulus (STIM-yuh-luhs)**:** Anything in the environment that causes a reaction or response. A hunting dog will respond to the stimulus of a nearby bird.

LEARN

Activity 1: Behaviors *(Online)*

Activity 2: Pill Bug Behaviors *(Offline)*

How do pill bugs respond to temperature changes and touch? Study data collected during an experiment with pill bug behavior and find out.

Activity 3: Optional: Alternate Activity: Pill Bug Behaviors *(Offline)*

How do pill bugs respond to temperature changes and touch? Use live pill bugs to test these stimuli and observe the pill bug behavior.

ASSESS

Lesson Assessment: Animal Behavior *(Offline)*

You will complete an offline assessment covering the main objectives of this lesson. Your learning coach will score this assessment.

LEARN

Activity 4: Optional: Habit Forming Behavior *(Offline)*

You have many behaviors, from brushing your teeth each night to blinking your eyes in sudden bright light. Can you re-learn or change a behavior you have already learned?

Name _____   Date _____

Animal Behavior
Pill Bug Behaviors

Pill bugs live under logs, moist leaves, flower pots, outdoor pet dishes, bricks, and stones. They are omnivores that eat decaying plants and animals. Pill bugs breathe through gills.

EXPERIMENT 1

Ten pill bugs were placed on an aluminum foil tray. The tray was divided into three sections—A, B, and C as shown below. A bowl of warm water was placed at one end of the tray. A bowl of ice cubes was placed at the opposite end. The bugs were placed in section B.

The illustrations below show where the bugs were after 5 minutes and after 10 minutes.

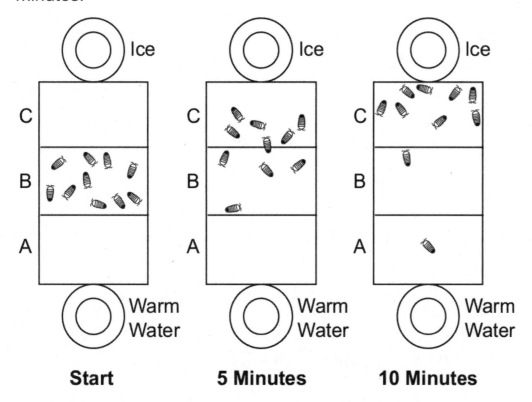

The chart shows where the pill bugs were at the end of 10 minutes. The data below that shows two more trials of the same experiment.

Trial	Section A	Section B	Section C
1	1	1	8
2	0	3	7
3	0	1	9

1. Based on the information gathered, in what type of climate would a pill bug probably live? _____

2. Would you describe the pill bugs' behavior in this experiment as *innate* or *learned*? _____

3. How might this behavior help pill bugs survive?

    _____

    _____

EXPERIMENT 2

Five pill bugs were placed on a dish. They were then touched gently with a pencil. Study the illustration below to see how the bugs reacted.

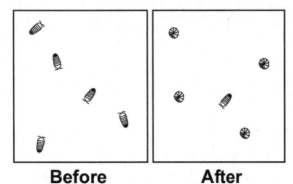

Before   **After**

4. What happened when the pill bugs were touched?

    _____

5. Would you describe this behavior as *innate* or *learned*? _____

6. How might this behavior help pill bugs survive?

    _____

    _____

Name _____   Date _____

Animal Behavior

Alternate Activity: Pill Bug Behaviors

Pill bugs live under logs, moist leaves, flower pots, outdoor pet dishes, bricks, and stones. They are omnivores who eat decaying plants and animals. Pill bugs breathe through gills.

EXPERIMENT 1

Procedure

1. Fold the edges of a sheet of aluminum foil to make a tray. Use a marker to divide the tray into three equal sections and label them A, B, and C.

2. Fill one bowl with warm water and another with ice cubes.

3. Place the bowl of ice at the C end of the tray and the warm water at the A end. Make sure the tray is touching the bowls.

4. Place 10 pill bugs into section B.

5. After 10 minutes, use the chart below to record how many pill bugs are in each section.

6. Repeat the experiment two more times with new ice cubes and warm water, and record your observations on the chart.

Data

Trial	Section A	Section B	Section C
1			
2			
3			

Analysis

1. Based on the information gathered, in what type of climate would a pill bug probably live?

   _____

2. Would you describe the pill bugs' behavior in this experiment as *innate* or *learned*? _____

3. How might this behavior help the pill bugs survive?

_____

_____

EXPERIMENT 2

1. Place five pill bugs in a dish.
2. Touch them gently with a pencil.

Analysis

1. What happens when you touch the pill bugs?

_____

2. Would you describe this behavior as *innate* or *learned*? _____

3. How might this behavior help the pill bugs survive?

_____

_____

Student Guide

Plant and Animal Interactions: Unit Review and Assessment

Review what you've learned by studying some interactions taking place in a national park. Match important words you have learned with their definitions. Show what you know by taking the Unit Assessment.

Lesson Objectives

- Identify behaviors as innate or learned.
- Classify organisms as predators and prey.
- Describe factors that affect the growth of a population.
- Explain that an animal's behavior helps it survive.
- Explain that living things cause changes in their ecosystems, and that some of these changes are detrimental to other organisms, and some are beneficial.
- Identify symbiotic relationships between organisms (mutualism, commensalism, and parasitism).
- Recognize that organisms in an ecosystem can compete for resources such as food, shelter, and water.
- State that a population is a group of individuals of the same type living in a certain area.

PREPARE

Approximate lesson time is 60 minutes.

Materials

For the Student

> Vocabulary Review Concentration
> pencil
> Brewster Ridge National Park

LEARN

Activity 1: Vocabulary Review Concentration *(Offline)*

Symbiosis, population density, behavior, stimulus. See how many keywords you can remember about plant and animal interactions.

Activity 2: Brewster Ridge National Park *(Offline)*

What kinds of plants and animals are found in Brewster Ridge National Park? Learn about some of the populations found there and how they interact.

ASSESS

Unit Assessment: Plant and Animal Interactions *(Offline)*

Complete an offline Unit Assessment. Your learning coach will score the assessment.

Name _____   Date _____

Plant and Animal Interactions: Unit Review and Assessment

Vocabulary Review Concentration

Cut out each word card and definition card. Lay them face down. With a partner, take turns trying to find matching words and definitions. If you find a match, you get another turn. The player with the most matches wins.

sampling	migration	immigration	emigration
competition	predator	prey	symbiosis
mutualism	parasitism	commensalism	behavior
stimulus	innate	imprinting	social behavior

the process of observing or counting a small part of a population as an indicator of the whole	a regular, usually long-distance movement of animals to a different location	movement or migration into a population	movement or migration out of a population
the struggle between two or more organisms or two or more kinds of organisms for resources in short supply	an animal that hunts for food	an animal or plant that is hunted for food	a relationship between two different kinds of organisms that live together in a way that benefits at least one of them
a symbiotic relationship in which both types of organisms help each other and both benefit	a symbiotic relationship in which one organism benefits and the other is harmed	a symbiotic relationship when one organism benefits and the other neither benefits nor is harmed	the way in which an organism responds to its environment
anything in the environment that causes a reaction or response	a type of behavior that is "built in" or does not have to be learned	developing behaviors during a specific period of time	any interaction between organisms of the same king

Name _____   Date _____

Plant and Animal Interactions: Unit Review and Assessment

Brewster Ridge National Park

Have you ever visited a national park? The difference between these parks and other recreation areas is that national parks protect the plants and animals that live there. Humans are not allowed to disturb anything in a national park, although they can visit the park to enjoy its resources.

To stay healthy, the plants and animals in national parks need care and attention. Below is part of a newspaper article about something that is happening to a group of animals in Brewster Ridge National Park. Use your knowledge about plant and animal interactions to answer some questions about the animals.

Bison and Brucellosis—A Dangerous Relationship: "Declines in bison, elk, and cattle possible," says expert.

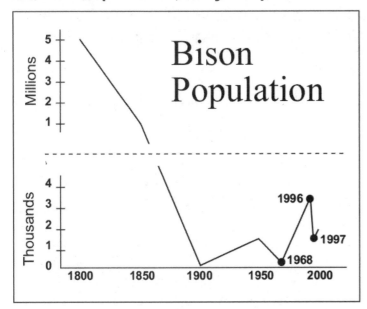

The bison, also called a buffalo, is a herd animal that can grow up to 6 feet tall and weigh as much as 1 ton. Bison have lived at Brewster Ridge for almost 200 years. During that time, the number of bison in the area has changed. In the early 1800s, the bison population numbered in the millions only to fall quickly into the thousands. The bison population is now stable—it does not change much anymore. Brewster Ridge National Park has no fences to keep the bison inside the park. They can wander into areas where people live, and they sometimes do damage to fences, crops, and yards. Bison are dangerous wild animals.

Some bison in Brewster Ridge are infected with a type of bacteria that causes a disease called brucellosis (broo-suh-LOH-suhs). Brucellosis harms female bison that are about to give birth. There is no cure for the disease, and people are worried that it may be passed on to the cattle and elk in the area.

1. What animal population is this article about? _____

2. Study the population graph.

   (a) During what time were bison hunted almost to extinction? _____

   (b) When do you think laws were passed to protect the bison in Brewster Ridge? _____

   (c) In 1954, the bison population had grown. Some bison were shipped out to live on other land. What happened to the bison population in Brewster Ridge? Is this an example of *immigration* or *emigration*?

   _____

   (d) In the late 1980s, Brewster Ridge had very mild winters. How did this affect the bison population? What happened during a tough winter in 1996?

   _____

   _____

   _____

3. What kind of symbiotic relationship exists between bison and the bacteria that causes brucellosis: mutualism, commensalism, or parasitism?

   _____

To: Brewster Ridge National Park

From: Brewster Ridge Fisheries

Subject: Lake Trout

Dear Park Manager,

I am writing this letter from the Brewster Ridge Fisheries. We are very worried about the growing population of lake trout in Brewster Ridge Lake.

Years ago, lake trout were brought into Brewster Ridge Lake by someone who wanted to improve fishing. Unfortunately, lake trout are a threat to another kind of fish, cutthroat trout. Young lake trout compete with cutthroat trout for food. Adult lake trout prey on cutthroat trout.

Losing cutthroat trout would affect other animals. Pelicans, otters, black bears, minks, ospreys, and loons feed on cutthroat trout. So do bald eagles and grizzly bears—animals who are in danger of dying out themselves.

You might think that these animals could just eat lake trout. Lake trout live in very deep water, and so are impossible to catch. Fishermen do not have good equipment for catching lake trout, either.

If the lake trout population keeps growing, cutthroat trout fisheries will lose money. It is important for park managers to study lake trout and keep their population from growing.

Sincerely,

Bob F. Macmillan

Fisherman

4. Name three populations discussed in the letter.

   _____

   _____

5. Lake trout caused changes in the ecosystem. Was this a good change or a bad change? Why?

   _____

   _____

6. List the predators of the cutthroat trout.

   _____

   _____

7. Are the mammals and birds in Brewster Ridge Lake competing for food, water, or shelter? How will the competition affect them?

   _____

   _____

8. Can the mammals and birds in Brewster Ridge Lake adapt to the growing population of lake trout?

   _____

My Trip to Brewster Ridge National Park

By Marion Rhodes

This weekend I went to visit Brewster Ridge National Park. We talked to a ranger. He told us a lot about one of the park's favorite residents—the black bear.

He said that only black bears live in the park, and that brown and cinnamon bears live in other places. Black bears eat berries, nuts, animals, and insect larvae. They can see colors, and they have an excellent sense of smell.

Bears are active during the spring and summer, and during early morning and late evening. In the winter, a bear chooses a den. Then the bear becomes very sleepy. Its body temperature drops and its heartbeat and breathing slow down. The bear eats extra food to store as fat for energy before it enters a special, very deep sleep. This is called *hibernating*.

The ranger told us **NOT** to feed the bears. Bears can smell food and will take it from a person's hand. This teaches the bear to not be afraid of humans. It also turns wild, healthy bears into "beggars." These bears can damage property and hurt people. They also do not live as long as wild bears. They may be hit by cars or die from eating food packaging.

You should watch bears from a safe distance. If a bear senses danger, it will make a low, grunting noise. If a bear comes near, you should move away from it slowly.

9. List the behaviors of the black bear you read about in the report.

_____

_____

_____

_____

10. Which behaviors are innate? Which are learned?

_____

_____

_____

Student Guide

Working Together

The human body is a miracle of efficiency. Our body systems all keep us alive, from the ones that allow us to move to those that fight disease. Scientists have studied these systems in detail, using specific terms so we can all communicate about them. Let's examine what they have found and see what makes the human body so remarkable.

The human body is made up of millions of tiny cells. Groups of cells make tissues. Groups of tissues make organs. Groups of organs make systems, and groups of systems make up our body. Each system has a specific task and yet all systems have to work together to make our bodies run smoothly.

Lesson Objectives

- Define a body system as cells, tissues and organs working together to perform a certain job.
- Identify the various body systems and their functions.
- Describe the five senses and their related sensory organs.

PREPARE

Approximate lesson time is 60 minutes.

Materials

For the Student

> Body Systems Review
> pencil
> Overload!
> timer - stopwatch

Keywords and Pronunciation

adrenal (uh-DREE-nl)

cell: The basic unit of all living things.

cytoplasm (SIY-tuh-pla-zuhm)

endocrine (EN-duh-kruhn)

hormone: A substance that is released by the endocrine glands and travels through the blood to influence other glands and organs

organ: A body part that does a special job within a body system. The heart is the organ that pumps blood through your body.

pancreas (PAN-kree-uhs)

pineal (PIY-nee-uhl)

pituitary (puh-TOO-uh-tair-ee)**:** A gland found at the base of the brain, responsible for making human growth hormone. The pituitary gland is the main gland responsible for growth.

system: A group of body parts that work together to perform a job. The main body systems are the nervous, skeletal, muscular, endocrine, respiratory, and circulatory systems.

tissue: a group of cells that are similar in structure and that work together to perform a certain function

vertebrae (VUR-tuh-bray)

LEARN

Activity 1: Many Systems, One Body *(Online)*

Activity 2: Body Systems Review *(Offline)*

Right now you might be thinking that your body is very complicated. There is a lot to learn about the many systems that make up the human body. Organizing what you've learned in a chart will help you remember.

Activity 3: Body Systems Overload *(Offline)*

All of your body systems are working together to keep you alive even when you are sitting still. What happens to them when you are running or jumping? Study how these systems respond when you attempt to overload them with exercise.

Safety

This activity involves a few minutes of strenuous physical activity.

ASSESS

Lesson Assessment: Working Together *(Offline)*

You will complete an offline assessment covering the main objectives of this lesson. Your learning coach will score this assessment.

LEARN

Activity 4: Optional: Find Out More: Body Systems *(Online)*

You can never run out of things to find out about the human body. Any scientist will tell you that human body systems are studied all the time in order to cure diseases or repair injuries.

You will be doing a web search to learn more. Web searches should always be done with adult supervision. K12 recommends the use of the safe search options that most web browsers come with, or one of the safe search engines produced by many major search engine providers.

Find more about this topic. Search for these key terms:

- kids health body systems

Safety

As usual, you may wish to preview the websites listed in this lesson.

Note: The second website suggested in this activity has a reference to the reproductive system.

Name _____ Date _____

Working Together
Body Systems Review

Use information from the Explore section to complete the chart.

System Name	Function	Parts	Without this system, I could not…
Nervous			
Skeletal and Muscular			
Respiratory			
Circulatory			
Endocrine			

Name _____ Date _____

Working Together

Overload!

The systems in your body are working all of the time. Even as you sit and read, your nervous system is sending signals from your eyes to your brain. These signals help to figure out how the letters make words and to understand what they mean. Your heart is beating, you are breathing air into your lungs, and your skeleton and muscles are supporting your body.

These systems respond to any changes you make in your body. They even respond to small ones such as scratching an itch or flexing your toes. When you are very active, you can feel these systems working to keep up with your body's changes.

Materials:

stopwatch

Procedure

1. For the next few minutes do the following exercises:

   - Touch your toes 20 times.
   - Jog in place for 2 minutes.
   - Do 30 jumping jacks.

2. Answer the questions immediately after you are finished.

Observations:

During your exercise, did you detect any changes in your body? How did your systems respond? Could you feel all of them responding? Fill in the table with your observations. One is done for you.

System	Response	Could you feel the response?
Nervous	My nervous system told my muscles and bones how to move, counted the exercises and kept time, and told me when to stop.	No
Skeletal and Muscular		
Circulatory		
Respiratory		
Endocrine		

1. Can you feel the response of every body system in your body?

_____

_____

2. Which body system responses can YOU control?

_____

3. Do your body systems respond when you are sleeping? How?

_____

_____

Fact:

With more exercise, certain body systems can learn and respond in ways that make you stronger and healthier. For example, your muscles become stronger and you can exercise longer. Your heart becomes more efficient at pumping blood and delivering oxygen to your cells. Your lungs can take in more oxygen with every breath. Exercise is good for body systems!

Student Guide

Under Control: Your Nervous System

We need all our body systems working in order to live, but the nervous system is the one in charge. It controls our thoughts, movements, and reactions. It is also the center of our senses. It allows us to see, feel, hear, smell, and taste. Learn how our nervous system works and how it compares to the nervous systems of other life forms.

Lesson Objectives

- Compare the voluntary nervous system with the involuntary nervous system.
- Define a reflex as movements that happen very quickly without your thinking about them.
- Describe the five senses and their related sensory organs.
- Describe the function of the nervous system and identify its parts.
- Explain how neurons carry impulses throughout the body.
- Develop a model to describe that light reflecting from objects and entering the eye allows objects to be seen.

PREPARE

Approximate time is 60 minutes.

Materials

For the Student

> Keep Your Brain in Shape
> Inside the Eye Assignment

Optional

> coins
> cups
> toothbrush
> voice recording device

Keywords and Pronunciations

brain: The control center of the body. The brain tells your body what to do.

nerve: Bundles of axons that are found throughout the body. There are many nerves in hands.

reflex: A movement that happens very quickly, without your thinking about it. When you touch something hot, your hand pulls away quickly in a reflex action.

spinal cord: A thick bundle of nerves that runs up and down the inside of the spine, or backbone. The spinal cord is located inside the backbone.

vertebrae (VUR-tuh-bray)

LEARN

Activity 1: Structure of the Nervous System *(Online)*

Activity 2: The Eyes Have It *(Online)*

Use your drawing to help explain how light reflects from an object, enters the eye and signals the brain.

Activity 3: Keep Your Brain in Shape *(Offline)*

Your five senses—sight, hearing, smell, touch, and taste—are like doorways to your brain for special kinds of information. Seeing and hearing can quickly tell you a lot about your environment. Think about what you can learn from magazines, television, computer screens, radio—and you only need two senses to do it! Try some of the exercises in this activity to make use of more of your senses.

ASSESS

Lesson Assessment: Under Control: Your Nervous System *(Offline)*

You will complete an offline assessment covering the main objectives of this lesson. Your learning coach will score this assessment.

Name _____ Date _____

Assignment

Inside the Eye

Use the information you have learned in this lesson to draw a model of the eye. You can complete this assignment on paper or with a computer program. Your picture should show how the light reflecting off an object travels through the eye and then to your brain.

Your drawing must include the following labels:

- Actual Image (what you are looking at)
- Eye
- Pupil
- Optic Nerve
- Image Seen by the Eye
- Final Image (what your brain tells you you're looking at)
- Brain
- Path of Light

Use your drawing to describe the path that light takes between reflecting off an object and being sent to the brain.

Name _____   Date _____

Under Control: Your Nervous System

Keep Your Brain in Shape

The brain loves having new experiences to understand. You might tie your shoes or ride a bike without thinking too much about it, but when you first learned these things, your brain had to work hard to get it right. New experiences make your brain work harder and stay in shape. Try some of these activities, and then read about what's happening in your brain when you do them.

1. Toothbrush Twist

Brush your teeth with the hand you use less often to do things. If you normally write, brush, eat, or use the remote with your left hand, switch to your right hand.

What's going on? Your right and left hands are controlled by the opposite sides of your brain. By switching the hand you use to do things, you are using parts in the side of the brain you don't normally use—and this makes those parts work hard! This kind of exercise can quickly grow the parts of your brain that understand information from your sense of touch.

2. Make Change

Fill a cup with different coins. Close your eyes and use your sense of touch to make different amounts of money. Have a friend give you an amount such as $1.00 or $0.65.

What's going on? We rely so much on sight that we sometimes ignore our sense of touch. Using touch to find the right coins makes those areas that understand touch work harder and become stronger.

3. Scramble Your Space

You probably have your work area organized a certain way. You may have markers and pencils on the left, scissors and a stapler on the right. Switch everything to a new location (ask permission first).

What's going on? Your brain has made an "internal map" of your work space. You can probably reach for things without even thinking about this map. By moving things around, your brain has to relearn your new space. Your sense of sight and touch must work to adjust the map in your brain.

4. Food Find

Next time you go to the grocery store, make a list of foods to buy based on their description, not their names (or have someone make one for you). For example, "It's oblong and yellow, and has a stem on the end."

What's going on? Whether you make the list or someone makes the list for you, you will be using different ways of "seeing" the food you're looking for.

5. Pinch Your Nose

Most of what you call taste depends on your sense of smell. To see how much, next time you eat, pinch your nose closed.

What's going on? Your taste buds sense sweet, salt, sour or bitter, astringent, and metallic taste. Pinching your nose keeps you from picking up the flavor of your food. Your brain must use different pathways to understand what you are eating.

6. Name That Sound

Record sounds you normally hear at home or at play. Play the sounds back for friends or family, and see if they can name each sound and what's making it. You can also use a sound-effects CD or sounds downloaded from the computer.

What's going on? Your brain already has large paths for understanding things you see. By relying on your sense of hearing to name things, you'll be making those pathways stronger, too.

Training your brain is a fun and healthy way to keep it active and working. Seek out new experiences whenever you can, and you'll keep your brain in top shape.

Student Guide
Nerves

Nerves are connected throughout the body and the signals they send are constantly moving from one place to another. But how? The nerve cell, or *neuron*, has specialized parts that pass these messages along. Learn what these parts are and the jobs they carry out.

Lesson Objectives

- Explain how neurons carry impulses throughout the body.
- Identify the parts of a neuron and their functions.
- Name the three main parts of the brain: the cerebrum, cerebellum and brain stem.

PREPARE

Approximate lesson time is 60 minutes.

Advance Preparation

If you don't already have it, you will need pipe cleaners (five different colors) for the Model Neuron experiment.

Materials

For the Student

> Model Neuron
> pipe cleaners - five different colors
> scissors

Keywords and Pronunciation

axon: The long arm of a neuron that is responsible for conducting nerve impulses away from the cell body.

cell body: The central part of a neuron that contains the nucleus of the cell.

dendrite (DEN-driyt)**:** The tree-like, branching arms of a neuron, which usually conduct nerve impulses toward the body of the neuron.

glial (GLEE-uhl)

neuron: A nerve cell made up of three main parts: dendrites, a cell body and an axon.

synapse (SIH-naps)

LEARN

Activity 1: Impulse! *(Online)*

Activity 2: Model Neuron *(Offline)*

Learning about nerve cells is fun. Unfortunately, they are too small to be studied directly. Instead, make a model neuron to review its parts and how impulses travel between them.

ASSESS

Lesson Assessment: Nerves *(Offline)*

You will complete an offline assessment covering the main objectives of this lesson. Your learning coach will score this assessment.

Name _____ Date _____

Nerves

Model Neuron

When someone says, "Hey, you're getting on my nerves!" what exactly does that mean? Are you suddenly stepping on their axons? Blocking neurotransmitters in their synapses? You might want to ask because you know that most neurons are really too small for someone to get on them in the first place.

You can understand what a nerve cell looks like by making a model with pipe cleaners.

Materials:

five pipe cleaners of different colors

scissors

Step 1	Step 2	Step 3	Step 4	Step 5	Step 6

Procedure:

1. Take one pipe cleaner, of any color, and roll it into a coil. This is the cell body of your nerve.

2. Take another pipe cleaner and fold it in half. Poke the ends through the center of the cell body and pull them all the way through so the two halves are sticking out. Take the two halves and twist them together into a single twisted pipe cleaner. This is the axon.

3. Take a third pipe cleaner and carefully cut it into a few pieces.

4. Push the small pieces of pipe cleaner through the cell body. You can twist them. These are your dendrites.

5. Wrap a fourth pip cleaner along the length of the axon. This is the fatty sheath covering the cell.

6. Wrap the last pipe cleaner on the end of the axon opposite the cell body. This is the synaptic terminal. On the other side of it would be a synapse.

Questions:

1. Fill in the table describing the job of each part of a neuron.

Part	Job
cell body	
axon	
dendrites	
fatty sheath	
synaptic terminal	

2. Below is a description of how nerve impulses travel from one neuron to another. Number them in order from one to five. Use your model if you need to.

_____ Neurotransmitters stimulate the dendrites of the next neuron.

_____ Electrical signals in the dendrites are sent to the nerve cell body.

_____ At the end of the axon, neurotransmitters are released into the synapse.

_____ A nerve impulse travels down the axon of the neuron.

_____ The nerve cell body receives the impulse.

Student Guide

The Cerebrum, Cerebellum, and Brain Stem

Studying the brain is thinking about how you think. The brain is made of three major parts, which are responsible for all its functions. Study the cerebellum, cerebrum, and brain stem. Make a life-size model of the brain and get to know a funny little guy called *homunculus*.

Lesson Objectives

- Name the three main parts of the brain: the cerebrum, cerebellum and brain stem.

PREPARE

Approximate lesson time is 60 minutes.

Advance Preparation

- You will need instant potato flakes for this science activity.

Materials

For the Student

> Centimeter Grid Paper
> Map the Homunculus
> ruler, metric
> toothpicks (2)
> food - instant potatoes (360 ml)
> sand - 2 cups (480 ml)
> bags, zipper-close - gallon size
> water - hot, 2.5 cups (600 ml)

Keywords and Pronunciation

cerebellum (sehr-uh-BEH-luhm)**:** The portion of the hindbrain that helps to control posture, balance, and motor coordination.

cerebral (suh-REE-bruhl)

cerebrum (suh-REE-bruhm)

corpus callosum (KOR-puhs ka-LOH-suhm)**:** The bundle of nerve fibers that connects the left and right hemispheres of the brain.

glial (GLEE-uhl)

homunculus (hoh-MUHN-kyuh-luhs)**:** A sensory map of the body.

occipital (ahk-SIH-puh-tl)

parietal (puh-RIY-uh-tl)

temporal (TEM-pruhl)

LEARN

Activity 1: The Thinking Brain *(Online)*

Activity 2: Map the Homunculus *(Online)*

Now that you know what a homunculus is, make one of your own. Using a two-point touch test, you can explore the places on your body that have the most sensory receptors.

On the next screen, you will find an online calculator to help you with parts of this activity.

Activity 3: Model Brain *(Offline)*

Albert Einstein's brain has been the subject of many brain studies. But what is a brain like close up? Make a life-size model that even feels like a real brain.

Materials:

instant potato flakes 360 ml

hot water 600 ml

clean sand 2 cups (480 ml)

1 gallon plastic zipper-close bag

Procedure:

Combine all of the ingredients in the plastic bag and mix thoroughly. It should weigh about 1.5 kg (3 lbs) and feel like a real brain.

If you are interested in brain studies, this model gives you a good idea of what a brain looks and feels like. Show your brain to others and let them know just how "brain-like" it is. See if anyone thinks it's a real brain.

ASSESS

Lesson Assessment: The Cerebrum, Cerebellum, and Brain Stem *(Offline)*

You will complete an offline assessment covering the main objectives of this lesson. Your learning coach will score this assessment.

Name _____   Date _____

Centimeter Grid Paper

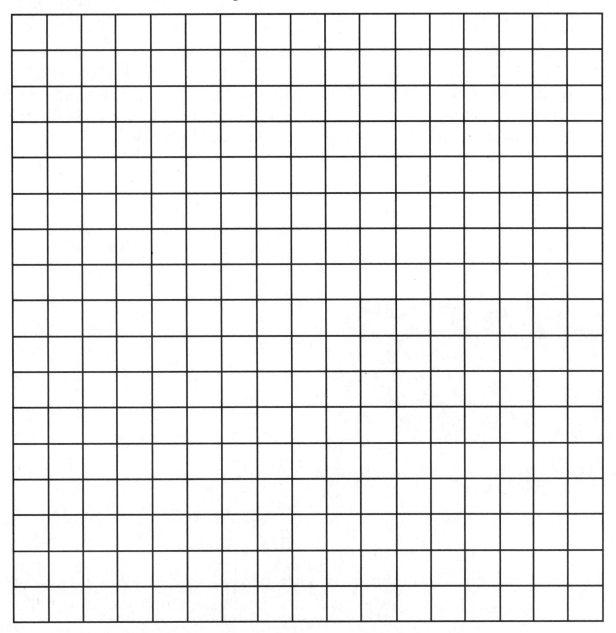

Name _____   Date _____

The Cerebrum, Cerebellum, and Brain Stem
Map the Homunculus

The odd-looking homunculus helps us understand how sense receptors are distributed in the body. Each body part is drawn based on the number of sense receptors found there, not on its size. That's why the hands, tongue, and lips are very large and the forehead and knees are not. You can perform a simple touch test to see if the homunculus describes sense receptors in your body.

Materials:

two toothpicks

graph paper

ruler

calculator

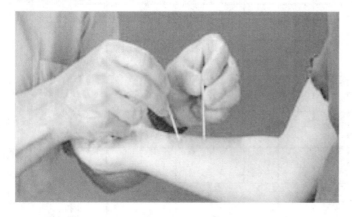

Procedure:

To do the test, you will need a partner.

1. As you look away, have your partner gently touch two toothpicks to the skin of your right forearm as shown. Make sure both toothpicks touch your arm at the same time.

2. You should feel two points of contact. If not, have your partner move the toothpicks farther apart until you do.

3. Lift and move the toothpicks closer together, about 0.5 cm at a time, until you no longer can tell there are two toothpicks touching you. Instead, it should feel like just one toothpick. This means both toothpicks touching your arm are being sensed by the same touch receptor.

4. Measure and record the distance between the two toothpicks and record it in the table. Round to the nearest tenth of a centimeter.

5. Repeat steps one through four on the right side of your body for the other parts listed.

Body Part – Right Side	Distance between toothpicks in cm	Size on graph paper
forehead		
cheek		
lips		
nose		
upper arm		
lower arm		
palm		
elbow		
fingertips		
shoulder		
kneecap		
calf		
sole		
toes		

Analysis:

1. Be sure to have a calculator nearby to get ready to draw the homunculus. If you do not have one, an online calculator has been provided for you.

2. The closer the receptors are in your tests, the larger they will need to be on the homunculus. You need to find what's called an "inverse" to figure out just how large the part should be.

3. Divide all of your measurements into the number 1. Example: Distance = 0.2; 1 ÷ 0.2 = 5. This means this body part will be as large as 5 boxes on graph paper.

4. Write your answer in the "Size on Graph Paper" column.

5. Repeat steps two through four for all measurements.

6. Use the measurements in the "Size on Graph Paper" column to draw a picture of your homunculus on graph paper. Do the best you can to make a normal body shape!

Conclusions:

1. Which part of the brain is responsible for interpreting touch?

   _____

2. Which side of your body did you test? _____ Which side of the brain's sensory cortex did you map? Explain.

   _____

   _____

3. How does your homunculus compare to the one you saw in the lesson?

   _____

   _____

   _____

   _____

Interesting fact:

Animals have a homunculus! (Since the Latin word for person is "homo," perhaps an animal would have an "animunculus.") Think about how the homunculus might look for rats, rabbits, or giraffes. How might a giraffe homunculus look if there are a small amount of sensory receptors in its neck?

Student Guide
Optional: More About the Brain/Other Brain Structures

Studying the brain is a challenge. With special equipment, though, scientists can begin to find out what all that gray matter does. They also learn a lot by studying the brains of other animals. Explore these techniques and the structures they reveal. Investigate what happens when you confuse your own brain. Learn about the brains of other animals, and be able to respond scientifically when you hear the words "bird brain"!

Lesson Objectives

- Identify the locations and describe some of the main functions of the cerebellum, brain stem, and the cerebrum.

PREPARE

Approximate lesson time is 60 minutes.

Materials

For the Student

> Brain Tricks
> blindfold
> household item - pillow
> markers

Keywords and Pronunciation

cerebellum (sehr-uh-BEH-luhm)**:** The portion of the hindbrain that helps to control posture, balance, and motor coordination.

cerebral (suh-REE-bruhl)

cerebrum (suh-REE-bruhm)

medulla oblongata (muh-DUH-luh ah-blahng-GAH-tuh)**:** The part of the brain that sends signals between the left and right sides of the brain in vertebrates. The medulla oblongata contains areas that control breathing.

meninges (muh-NIN-jeez)**:** A membrane that surrounds the brain and spinal cord in vertebrates. The brain surgeon had to cut through the meninges to get to the brain.

pons: A portion of the brainstem that is involved in coordinating muscular action and facial expressions.

thalamus (THA-luh-muhs)**:** The part of the brain that sends signals to the cerebral cortex. The thalamus is located in the lower part of the brain.

LEARN

Activity 1: Optional: Lesson Instructions (*Online*)

This lesson is OPTIONAL. It is provided for students who seek enrichment or extra practice. You may skip this lesson.

If you choose to skip this lesson, then go to the Plan or Lesson Lists page and mark this lesson "Skipped" in order to proceed to the next lesson in the course.

Activity 2: Optional: Brainstorming (*Online*)

Safety

As usual, you may wish to preview the websites suggested in this lesson.

Activity 3: Optional: Brain Tricks (*Offline*)

Scientists who study brains will always have work to do. There is plenty of new information to find out about how the brain works. Now, try some simple tests, and observe the effects of tricking your brain into thinking in ways it's not used to.

Name _____ Date _____

More About the Brain/Other Brain Structures
Brain Tricks

How complicated our brains are. Everything you do involves a whole lot of brain, from the medulla oblongata to tiny little dendrites picking up signals from even tinier neurotransmitters. It's a wonder messages from the tips of our toes make it to the tops of our heads at all.

At your age, your brain has learned to accomplish many tasks, some simple and some not so simple. Explore the training of your brain as you attempt some not-so-ordinary tasks.

Test 1: That's Blue! Or Maybe it's Red.

The different parts of your brain have certain jobs and are responsible for certain kinds of information. One part of your cerebrum knows, and can say, colors when you see them. Another part of your cerebrum can read and write letters. This test investigates whether or not those two parts of your brain can work together without getting confused.

1. Gather six markers: green, red, orange, blue, yellow, purple.

2. Do the following:

With the…	Write the word…
green marker	purple
red marker	yellow
orange marker	blue
purple marker	orange
yellow marker	green
blue marker	red

Could you do it? Write if this was an easy or hard test to do.

_____

Test 2: Look, No Hands! (Woops!)

Although one day you might use your brain to be an aerospace engineer or molecular biology professor, today you are going to use it to stay balanced. Your brain is heavily involved in this seemingly simple task.

Deep in your ear are canals filled with liquid. Imagine turning a cup of water—the liquid moves around the sides of the cup, moving more slowly on one side than the other. When you move, the liquid in the canals moves too, eventually stimulating nerve cells that send signals to your brain, keeping you balanced.

Once you are balanced, changing your position causes movement, and this liquid moves, too. You are required to balance yourself all over again.

Find a partner to help you with this activity (and to catch you if you fall).

1. In a safe place with a soft floor, stand on a pillow. This confuses information from the pressure sensors in the skin of the soles of your feet. Balance yourself.

2. Stand on one foot. Now you only have half of the pressure information you had before.

3. Have your partner blindfold you. Now you cannot see things to tell if you are upright.

4. Hold your arms by your sides. Now you cannot swing your arms to help stay balanced as you move around.

5. Remove the blindfold.

Tell how easy or hard it was to stay balanced when you were on one foot, blindfolded, with your hands by your sides.

Test 3: I'm a Lefty. No, I'm a Righty!

The left side of your brain generally controls the right side of your body. The right side of your brain controls the left side of your body. These signals cross in the structure called the medulla oblongata. The medulla oblongata is like a complicated train station, sending signals from one side of your brain to the other.

You are used to using certain sides of your body for certain things. You may write with your left hand but hit a baseball right-handed. For a few minutes, try to do normal tasks with the opposite hand. You might try:

- drinking from a mug
- brushing your teeth
- writing a note
- throwing a ball
- talking on the phone
- using a computer mouse

See if you can do this for an entire day. How hard is it to untrain your brain this way?

Some people can use either hand for any task. These people are called "ambidextrous." Do you know anyone who is ambidextrous?

Student Guide
Spinal Cord and Nerves

In this lesson you will learn about the spinal cord and its functions. The spinal cord is a superhighway of nerve fibers. It is protected by the bones of the backbone. It carries electrical signals from all over the body to the brain and back again.

Lesson Objectives

- Describe how a nerve signal is transmitted through a reflex arc.
- Describe how the spinal cord helps in transmitting messages to and from the brain.
- State that the spine protects the spinal cord.

PREPARE

Approximate lesson time is 60 minutes.

Materials

For the Student

> Explore Your Reflexes
> cotton balls
> chair
> safety goggles
> Reaction Ruler
> ruler
> ruler, metric - meter stick

Keywords and Pronunciation

cerebrospinal (suh-ree-broh-SPIY-nl)

dorsal: Towards the back. A shark's dorsal fin can be seen sticking out of the water when the shark is swimming near the surface.

lateral nerves: Nerves that branch out from the spinal cord, containing many more branches to reach every nerve receptor in the body. Sometimes, as in the disease shingles, a single lateral nerve will become infected with a virus.

meninges (muh-NIN-jeez): A membrane that surrounds the brain and spinal cord in vertebrates. The brain surgeon had to cut through the meninges to get to the brain.

reflex: Movements that happen very quickly without your thinking about them. Pulling your hand back after touching a hot stove is a reflex action.

ventral: To the front. The man on the beach was lying on his ventral side—on his stomach; the sun was therefore striking his dorsal side warming up his back.

vertebrae (VUR-tuh-bray)

vertebrate (VUR-tuh-bruht): An animal with a backbone. Mammals, fish, and birds are classified as vertebrates because they have a backbone.

LEARN

Activity 1: Functions of the Spinal Cord *(Online)*

Activity 2: Reflex Exploration *(Offline)*

Have you ever shivered at the cold or gotten goose bumps when you were scared? If so, you've experienced a reflex. Test your reflexes and review how reflex messages are sent within your nervous system.

Activity 3: Reaction Ruler *(Offline)*

Are you a quick reactor or a signal slowpoke? Investigate the reaction speed of one of your friends. Afterwards, you may want to try the test on several people to find the quickest reactor around.

ASSESS

Lesson Assessment: Spinal Cord and Nerves *(Offline)*

You will complete an offline assessment covering the main objectives of this lesson. Your learning coach will score this assessment.

Name _____   Date _____

Spinal Cord and Nerves
Explore Your Reflexes

Test 1: The Knee-Jerk Reflex

Materials:

chair

cotton ball

safety goggles

Procedure:

1. Sit in a chair.

2. Cross your legs so your lower knee fits snugly into the back of your upper knee.

3. Have a partner tap your knee firmly with the edge of his open hand on the soft part just below the kneecap.

4. Does your leg twitch? You may need to practice with your partner to find the right site.

What Happens:

When your knee is tapped, signals travel from stretch sensors in your knee to your spinal cord and then back to the leg muscles. At the same time, other signals travel up the spinal cord to touch centers of the brain. You are aware that your leg moved, but it's usually too late to stop it from moving. That's how fast a reflex is.

Test 2: Blinking

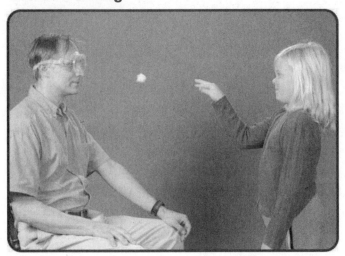

Procedure:

1. Have a partner sit in the chair and put on the safety googles.

2. Make sure you can see your partner's eyes through the safety goggles.

3. Stand about one meter away from your partner.

4. Without letting your partner know it's coming, throw a cotton ball directly at your partner's face. The goggles will protect your partner's eyes.

What Happens:

Your partner will blink and may jerk away or try to protect his eyes with his hands. Blinking is a reflex. Sense receptors in your eyes send messages to the spinal cord and brain. The signal is then passed to the muscles, resulting in movements to protect your eyes, such as blinking, moving, or raising a hand.

Review:

Below are the actions that take place in a reflex arc. Number them in order from one to five.

____ The signal stimulates a muscle that moves in response.

____ The signal does *not* go to your brain. It moves in a small loop around your spinal cord.

____ A nerve ending is stimulated and sends a signal up a nerve.

____ The signal enters your backbone through a dorsal connection.

____ Sense receptors react to something, such as touching something hot.

With all those steps, it is easy to forget just how quickly it all takes place. Involuntary reflexes take milliseconds. The fastest impulses can reach 320 miles per hour.

Name _____   Date _____

Spinal Cord and Nerves
Reaction Ruler

For your body to respond to a change, signals about the change must be sensed and interpreted by your nervous system. Then a message is sent through your nerves to your body, instructing it to respond. The time it takes for your body to react to messages from the brain is called reaction time. But how long is reaction time?

Materials:

ruler (or meter stick)

Procedure:

1. With one hand, hold the ruler at the 30-cm end with the 1-cm end hanging down. Raise your arm as high as possible in the air.

2. Have your partner face you. Have him place his thumb and index finger at the bottom of the ruler, but not touching it. The ruler should be able to slip through his hand.

3. Instruct your partner to catch the ruler as fast as possible after you let go.

4. Drop the ruler at any time without warning. Your partner should try to catch the ruler between his thumb and index finger.

5. Use the centimeter mark covered by your partner's finger to measure the distance the ruler fell before it was caught.

6. Repeat steps one through five several times. Can your partner change the distance it takes her to catch it?

What Happens:

Your partner will catch the ruler after it falls a small distance. This distance can be used to figure out your partner's reaction time. Reaction time is the time it takes for a message to travel from the brain to the muscles in the body to cause movement.

Review:

Teach your partner about what happened by doing and saying the following:

> *[Point to your partner's eyes and head.]* "In this test, electrical signals from sense receptors in your eyes are sent to lateral nerves, the spinal cord, and then finally the brain."
>
> *[Point to your partner's back, head and the ruler.]* "The signal is sent by a dorsal connection to the correct part of your brain, which realizes the ruler is falling."
>
> *[Point to your partner's arm, thumb, and index finger.]* "You decide to catch the ruler, and messages are sent through the ventral connection to the spinal cord, lateral nerves, and finally the muscles in your arm, thumb, and index finger."

Investigation Idea:

Try the same test with your partner's eyes closed. Say "go" when the ruler is dropped. How did reaction time change?

Have several friends or family members try this activity. Do some people have faster reaction times than others? You may want to test older and younger people as well.

Student Guide

Endocrine System: Glands and Hormones

The *endocrine system* is another one of the body's control systems. It works by putting out special chemicals called *hormones*. The hormones are produced in one part of the body and act in another. Learn about these hormones and how they control many of your body's activities.

Lesson Objectives

- Describe how glands and their hormones affect body processes.
- Identify the major glands in the endocrine system and describe their functions.
- State that the endocrine system is made up of glands and hormones that function over different amounts of time.

PREPARE

Approximate lesson time is 60 minutes.

Materials

For the Student

> The Endocrine System
> Feedback Mechanisms

Keywords and Pronunciation

adrenal (uh-DREE-nl)

adrenaline (uh-DREH-nl-uhn)

cretinism (KREE-tn-ih-zuhm)

endocrine (EN-duh-kruhn)

endocrine system (EN-duh-kruhn): A body system made up of glands and hormones that work with the nervous system. The endocrine system is one of the body's control systems.

gland: An organ that produces chemicals that perform special jobs in the body. The thyroid gland produces a chemical called thyroxine.

hormone: A chemical produced by glands and released into the bloodstream. Hormones are produced in one part of the body but affect a different part.

hypoglycemia (hiy-poh-gliy-SEE-mee-uh)

islets of Langerhans (IY-luhts of LAHNG-uhr-hahnts)

medulla: One of two tissue types found in the adrenal glands. This tissue is reponsible for producing adrenaline and noradrenaline.

pancreas (PAN-kree-uhs)

pituitary (puh-TOO-uh-tair-ee): A gland found at the base of the brain, responsible for making human growth hormone. The pituitary gland is the main gland responsible for growth.

thyroxine (thiy-RAHK-seen)

LEARN

Activity 1: Glands at Work *(Online)*

Safety

As usual, you may wish to preview the websites listed in this lesson.

Note: the website suggested in this activity has a reference to the reproductive glands.

Activity 2: The Great Regulator: The Endocrine System *(Offline)*

The endocrine system is responsible for sending important messages inside your body. It does this through chemicals called *hormones*. Review the major parts of the endocrine system and their functions.

Activity 3: Feedback Mechanisms: Message Received *(Offline)*

Without hormones our bodies could go into shock, or even dry out. Your body is so smart it detects and adjusts to changes without your realizing it. Learn about how your body responds to some common changes you face every day.

ASSESS

Lesson Assessment: Endocrine System: Glands and Hormones *(Online)*

You will complete an online assessment covering the main objectives of this lesson. Your assessment will be scored by the computer.

Name _____   Date _____

Endocrine System: Glands and Hormones
The Endocrine System

Use the word bank to label the main glands of the endocrine system. Then fill in the blanks to describe their functions.

Word Bank

brain   thyroid   pancreas

adrenal glands   pituitary gland

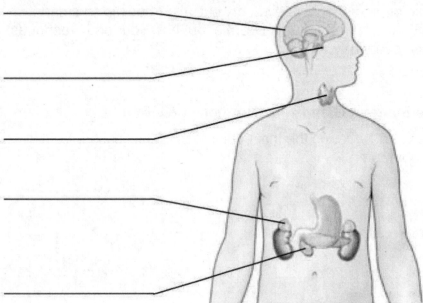

1. Insulin, a hormone that regulates sugar uptake, is produced in the

    _____.

2. This gland, called the _____, makes thyroxine, which is involved in growth.

3. The _____ is often called the "*master gland*" because it produces so many different hormones.

4. The organ that gives orders to glands to release hormones is the

    _____.

5. Located on the kidneys, the _____ make adrenaline, which helps the body respond to fear.

Name _____ Date _____

Endocrine System: Glands and Hormones

Feedback Mechanisms

For you to carry out normal activities, certain factors inside your body must be regulated. These are things such as temperature, blood sugar, and water. It's dangerous for your body to get too hot, too cold, or too dry on the inside.

Your body stays regulated with the help of receptors and effectors. Receptors sense when something changes in your body. Effectors respond to the change. In other words, receptors send the message. Effectors say, "Message received!" and respond as needed. This process of sensing changes and adjusting to them is called a *feedback mechanism*. The levels of hormones in the body are controlled by feedback mechanisms.

Why are feedback mechanisms important? They are necessary for survival. If you step outside on a very cold day, a feedback mechanism keeps your internal body temperature high. Feedback mechanisms help you adjust to a change in your environment.

Let's take a look at how some feedback mechanisms regulate your body.

Water Regulation

Your cells need a certain amount of water to carry out cell processes. Trace the path of this feedback mechanism below on the diagram.

- Receptors that detect changes in water concentration are located on the hypothalamus.
- A change in water concentration activates these receptors.
- The hypothalamus sends a message to the pituitary gland next to it.
- The pituitary gland puts out a hormone (ADH) that targets the kidneys.
- Then ADH gets to the kidneys. It causes changes, making the kidneys able to take in more or less water (as needed).
- A little ADH makes the kidneys take in less water to be released in the blood stream.
- Concentrated ADH makes the kidneys take in more water to be released in the blood stream.

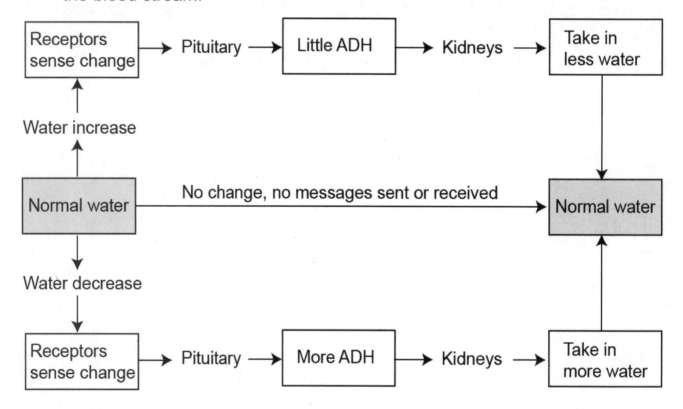

Blood Sugar Regulation

Your body needs certain levels of blood sugar to make energy. There are two hormones responsible for regulating blood sugar: insulin and glucagon. Trace the path of this feedback mechanism below on the diagram.

- A change in blood sugar switches on receptors in the pancreas.
- The pancreas puts out two types of hormones: insulin and glucagon.
- More insulin is released when blood sugar levels are high.
- More glucagon is released when blood sugar levels are low.
- Insulin and glucagon affect the liver.
- Insulin will cause the liver to store blood sugar instead of release it. Glucagon will cause the liver to produce new blood sugar and release it to cells.

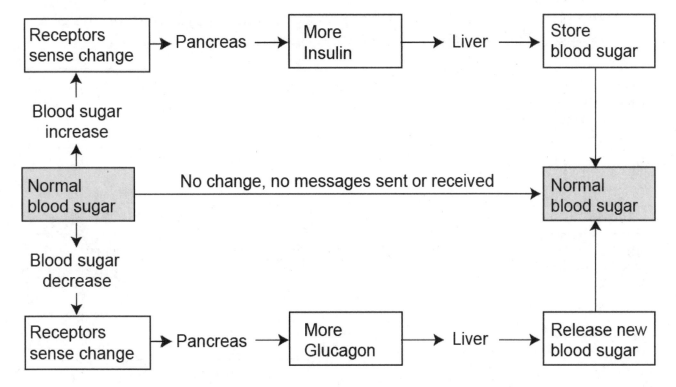

Temperature Regulation

Mammals and birds are able to regulate their body temperatures to adapt to their environments. This means that when they get too hot, their bodies react to cool them down. When they are too cold, their bodies respond in ways to keep them warm.

Read the steps involved in temperature regulation. Then, fill in the diagram.

- A change in temperature (increase or decrease) is sensed by receptors in the skin.
- The skin sends this information to the hypothalamus.
- The hypothalamus sends nerve impulses to the body.
- If the body is too hot, heat is released by sweating and by widening the blood vessels.
- If the body is too cold, heat is trapped by shivering, by tightening the blood vessels, and by making the hair stand on end.

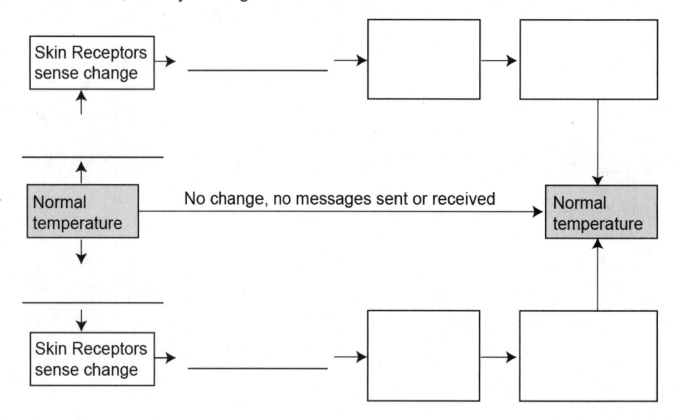

Review and Questions

Regulated levels of water, blood sugar, and temperature are necessary for your survival. Feedback mechanisms tell the body how to act by sending and receiving messages that bring about a response. Hormones are often very important in this process.

1. Tell which gland the following hormones come from.

    ADH _____

    Insulin _____

    Glucagon _____

2. Describe how each hormone keeps conditions of the body regulated.

    ADH

    _____

    _____

    _____

    Insulin

    _____

    _____

    _____

    Glucagon

    _____

    _____

    _____

3. Diabetes is a condition in which there is too much sugar in the blood. People who suffer from diabetes take injections of a certain hormone. Which hormone do you think they take? Why?

    _____

    _____

    _____

    _____

    _____

Student Guide

Optional: Growing Up

Growing up means a lot more than learning to behave like an adult. We also go through physical changes as we grow. The endocrine system plays a big part in this, especially the pituitary gland—the so-called *master gland*.

Lesson Objectives

- Describe aspects of a career in neuroscience.
- Describe how the pituitary gland affects human growth.

PREPARE

Approximate lesson time is 60 minutes.

Materials

For the Student

> paper, ruled
> pencil

Keywords and Pronunciation

acromegaly (a-kroh-MEH-guh-lee)**:** A disease that causes excess growth. Andre the Giant was a wrestler who suffered from acromegaly.

cartilage (KAHR-tl-ij)

endocrine (EN-duh-kruhn)

pituitary (puh-TOO-uh-tair-ee)**:** A gland found at the base of the brain, responsible for making human growth hormone. The pituitary gland is the main gland responsible for growth.

puberty: a process controlled by the endocrine system in which changes occur in the body, usually between the ages of 11 and 14.

LEARN

Activity 1: Optional: Lesson Instructions (*Offline*)

This lesson is OPTIONAL. It is provided for students who seek enrichment or extra practice. You may skip this lesson.

If you choose to skip this lesson, then go to the Plan or Lesson Lists page and mark this lesson "Skipped" in order to proceed to the next lesson in the course.

Activity 2: Optional: How You Grow (*Online*)

Activity 3: Optional: Measuring Up (*Online*)

Did you know that former US president James Madison was only 5 feet 4 inches (123 cm) tall? This did not make him a bad president, just a shorter one compared to the other presidents.

Activity 3: Optional: Measuring Up *(Online)*

Did you know that former US president James Madison was only 5 feet 4 inches (123 cm) tall? This did not make him a bad president, just a shorter one compared to the other presidents.

Use a growth chart to compare your height to other children your age, and determine your rank among them.

Activity 4: Optional: Careers in Medicine *(Online)*

The research of doctors and scientists has provided a lot of information about how our bodies work. Study a day in the life of a neuroscientist. You can then provide advice to someone considering a neuroscience career of his or her own.

Student Guide

Optional: Daily Processes and Hormones

Have you ever begged for permission to stay up late and then fallen asleep anyway? We know that our bodies need to get sleep. But have you ever wondered why? Hormones in our body help control everything from when we sleep to when we get hungry. Learn more about how hormones help us digest the food we eat, keep our blood sugar regulated, and control how we sleep.

Lesson Objectives

- Describe the stages of the sleep-wake cycle.
- Explain how abnormalities in the hormone insulin, or in its use by the cells in the body, can cause diabetes.
- Explain how insulin and glucagon act in the regulation of blood sugar.
- Recognize that hormones play a role in controlling daily bodily processes like blood-glucose regulation, hunger, digestion, and the sleep-wake cycle.

PREPARE

Approximate lesson time is 60 minutes.

Materials

For the Student

    household item - clock
    paper, ruled
    pencil

Keywords and Pronunciation

adenosine (uh-DEE-nuh-seen)

ghrelin (GREH-lin)

glucagon (GLOO-kuh-gahn)

glycogen (GLIY-kuh-juhn)

insulin: A hormone produced in the pancreas that helps regulate blood-sugar levels. Our cat Patches has feline diabetes, so each morning I help my mother give him an insulin shot.

melatonin (meh-luh-TOH-nuhn)

orexin (uh-REHK-sin)

pancreas (PAN-kree-uhs)

pineal (PIY-nee-uhl)

prostaglandin (prahs-tuh-GLAN-duhn)

LEARN

Activity 1: Optional: Lesson Instructions (*Offline*)

This lesson is OPTIONAL. It is provided for students who seek enrichment or extra practice. You may skip this lesson.

If you choose to skip this lesson, then go to the Plan or Lesson Lists page and mark this lesson "Skipped" in order to proceed to the next lesson in the course.

Activity 2: Optional: Some Daily Dealings with Hormones (*Online*)

Activity 3: Optional: Sleep Experiments (*Online*)

Now that you have learned about the different stages of the sleep-wake cycle, try some experiments to learn more about your own sleep patterns.

Activity 4: Optional: Dealing with Diabetes (*Online*)

Visit the Juvenile Diabetes Research Foundation International to learn about diabetes and find out about people who live with diabetes everyday.

Go to the next screen to get started.

Student Guide

The Human Body: Unit Review and Assessment

The human body is an amazing and wonderful thing. You have learned a lot about all of the various body systems, and about all of the organs, tissues and cells that make them up. Use your knowledge to solve a mystery as you get ready to take the Unit Assessment.

Lesson Objectives

- Define senses, reflexes, voluntary nervous system, and involuntary nervous system.
- Describe that the brain gets information about the outside world and the rest of the body through nerves, and uses nerves to direct actions by other parts of the body.
- Explain that the endocrine system is composed of glands and chemical messengers called hormones, and they function over a wide range of time scales.
- Explain that the various systems of the human body function because the cells, tissues, and organs all work together.
- Identify locations of some major glands of the endocrine system (for example, adrenals, thyroid, pituitary, pancreas).
- Identify various parts of the nervous system (such as the brain, spinal cord, nerves, nerve cells, and neurotransmitters), along with their structures and functions.
- Compare the voluntary nervous system with the involuntary nervous system.
- Define a body system as cells, tissues and organs working together to perform a certain job.
- Define a reflex as movements that happen very quickly without your thinking about them.
- Describe the five senses and their related sensory organs.
- Identify the major glands in the endocrine system and describe their functions.
- Identify the parts of a neuron and their functions.
- Name the three main parts of the brain: the cerebrum, cerebellum and brain stem.
- State that the spine protects the spinal cord.

PREPARE

Approximate lesson time is 60 minutes.

LEARN

Activity 1: The Mysterious Organism *(Online)*

ASSESS

Unit Assessment: The Human Body *(Online)*

You will complete an online Unit Assessment covering the main objectives of this unit.

LEARN

Activity 2: Optional: ZlugQuest Measurement *(Online)*

Student Guide

Classifying Animals

What do a spotted ladybug, an octopus, and a sea urchin all have in common? These organisms are *invertebrates*—organisms that don't have a backbone. Meet other organisms and discover the world of invertebrates as you read *Come Learn With Me: Animals Without Backbones: Invertebrates*.

How are invertebrates different from vertebrates? How are they grouped in the Kingdom Animalia? Venture into the world of invertebrates and discover for yourself!

Lesson Objectives

- Explain that living things are sorted into different groups based on certain common characteristics.
- Recognize that invertebrates are not a single taxonomic group but are represented in many groups.
- State that *invertebrates* are organisms that do not have a backbone.
- State that *vertebrates* are organisms that have a backbone.

PREPARE

Approximate lesson time is 60 minutes.

Materials

For the Student

> *Come Learn with Me: Animals Without Backbones: Invertebrates* by Bridget Anderson

Keywords and Pronunciation

anemone (uh-NEH-muh-nee)

Arthropoda (AHR-thruh-pah-duh): The phylum of invertebrate animals, including insects and spiders, that have an exoskeleton, jointed legs, and a segmented body. More than 80 percent of all living species are arthropods.

Aurelia aurita (aw-REEL-ee-uh aw-RIY-tuh)

cell: The basic unit of all living things. There are many different types of cells in a living thing, each with a different job to do.

Chordata (kor-DAH-tuh)

classification: the process of dividing things into groups according to their characteristics

Cnidaria (niy-DAIR-ee-uh): The phylum of aquatic, invertebrate animals that includes jellyfish and sea anemones.

exoskeleton (EK-soh-skeh-luh-tuhn): The hard, outside body covering of an arthropod. The exoskeleton of the lobster protects the animal from predators in the ocean.

insect: An arthropod with three pairs of jointed legs and three body segments. Ants, grasshoppers, and mosquitoes are all insects.

---

invertebrate: An animal without a backbone. Sea stars, segmented worms, and spiders are classified as invertebrates because they don't have a backbone.

Kingdom Animalia: One of the six main groups into which all living things are divided. Most organisms in the animal kingdom are capable of movement, contain a nervous system, and take in food to produce energy.

phyla (FIY-luh)**:** Large groups of organisms that share similar characteristics. Phyla are the primary divisions within any kingdom. The singular of phyla is phylum.

phylogenetic (fiy-loh-juh-NEH-tihk)

species (SPEE-sheez)**:** A group of organisms that have many characteristics in common. The smallest and most specific groups that animals can be divided into are called species.

vertebrate (VUR-tuh-bruht)**:** An animal with a backbone. Mammals, fish, and birds are classified as vertebrates because they have a backbone.

LEARN

Activity 1: Let's Read! *(Online)*

What would your life be like if you didn't have a backbone? Ninety-five percent of animals on Earth don't have one. Learn about these animals and the world they inhabit.

Activity 2: Invertebrate Hunt *(Online)*

An *invertebrate* is an organism without a backbone. What invertebrates live near you?

Safety

As always, you may wish to preview any websites before your student views them.

ASSESS

Lesson Assessment: Classifying Animals *(Online)*

You will complete an online assessment covering the main objectives of this lesson. Your assessment will be scored by the computer.

Student Guide

The World of Sponges

Did you know that the original cleaning sponges were actually the skeletons of sponge animals? Enjoy the book and learn more about these fascinating creatures.

Lesson Objectives

- Identify characteristics of sponges (they have the ability to regenerate damaged parts, they reproduce through budding, and they live only in water).
- Identify the parts of a sponge (ostium, canal, osculum, and flagellum).

PREPARE

Approximate lesson time is 60 minutes.

Materials

For the Student

Come Learn with Me: Animals Without Backbones: Invertebrates by Bridget Anderson
Sponges

Keywords and Pronunciation

budding: A method of reproduction in which pieces of a sponge break off and develop into new sponges. A sponge produces many spores and regenerates through budding.

flagella (fluh-JEH-luh)**:** Tail-like structures on a cell that move back and forth. The flagella pushed the water through the canal of the sponge.

larva: The early life stage of certain animals that are not fully developed. When the egg of an insect hatches, the larva emerges.

osculum (AHS-kyuh-luhm)**:** A large pore through which filtered water leaves the body of a sponge. Sponges pump water through the canal of the sponge and out through the osculum.

ostium: The tiny pores, or holes, on the outer layer of a sponge. The ostium on the outer layer of the sponge allows water to enter into the canal of the sponge.

Porifera (paw-RIF-uhr-uh)**:** The phylum of the simple, invertebrate animals called sponges. The barrel sponge, vase sponge, and red beard sponge are part of the phylum Porifera.

regenerate: To grow back or repair parts that have been damaged. Sponges have the ability to regenerate body parts that may have been damaged by a predator.

spicules (SPIH-kyools)**:** Tiny fibers or minerals that make up the skeleton of a sponge. Within the jelly-like layer of a sponge cell is a network of needle-like spicules that form the skeleton of the sponge.

LEARN

Activity 1: Let's Read! *(Online)*

Sponges have a lot of practical uses, but the really interesting sponges aren't found in the kitchen or bathroom. Sponges live in oceans and other bodies of water, and they are living things that can move.

Activity 2: The Parts of a Sponge *(Online)*

Sponges have special features that make them unlike any other phylum. Investigate the parts of a sponge to discover how sponges are different from other organisms.

The sponge is an animal that has many different parts—each with a different job.

Use the book to label the parts of the sponge on the Sponge sheet. The labels for the parts of the sponge are in the Word Bank at the top of the sheet.

Then, below the picture, use the words to describe how water enters and exits the sponge's body cavity. You may use the book as a guide if you wish.

ASSESS

Lesson Assessment: The World of Sponges *(Online)*

You will complete an online assessment covering the main objectives of this lesson. Your assessment will be scored by the computer.

Name _____   Date _____

The World of Sponges
Sponges

1. Using the words in the Word Bank, label the parts of the sponge.

Word Bank

canal	osculum	spicule
flagella	ostia	

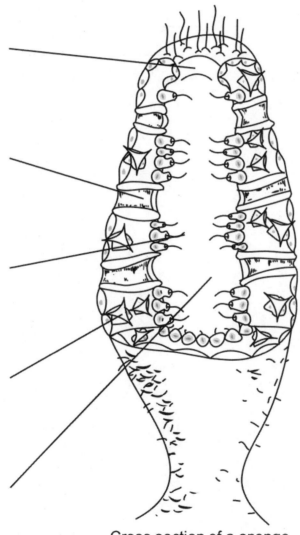

Cross section of a sponge

2. Use the words above to describe how water enters and exits the sponge's body cavity.

_____

_____

_____

_____

_____

_____

_____

Student Guide

Cnidarians

Have you ever been stung by a jellyfish? How are jellyfish able to do that? Learn more about the phylum Cnidaria, which includes interesting creatures such as jellyfish, sea anemones, and coral.

Lesson Objectives

- Identify a characteristic of cnidarians (they have tentacles with stinging cells).
- Identify medusa and polyp as the two common body types of cnidarians.
- Identify the three functions of tentacles (to sting predators, sense the environment, and bring food into the animal's mouth).
- State that most cnidarians help build up coral reefs.

PREPARE

Approximate lesson time is 60 minutes.

Materials

For the Student

> *Come Learn with Me: Animals Without Backbones: Invertebrates* by Bridget Anderson
> Cnidaria Descriptions

Keywords and Pronunciation

anemone (uh-NEH-muh-nee)

Cnidaria (niy-DAIR-ee-uh)**:** The phylum of aquatic, invertebrate animals that includes jellyfish and sea anemones.

medusa: A body form of cnidarians. Medusae float freely through the water.

mutualism (MYOO-chuh-wuh-lih-zuhm)**:** A relationship between two animals in which both animals benefit. Clownfish and sea anemones live together to help each other survive. This relationship is known as mutualism.

polyp (PAH-luhp)**:** A body form of cnidarians. A polyp attaches to rocks, shells, or the sea floor by its feet-like structures.

LEARN

Activity 1: Let's Read! *(Online)*

If you've spent a lot of time near oceans, you've probably seen cnidarians. You might also see them in rivers or lakes. Curious swimmers who come too close to these beautiful animals learn a lesson—cnidarians can defend themselves!

Activity 2: Characteristics of Cnidarians *(Online)*

Jellyfish, sea anemones, hydra, and corals are all cnidarians, but they have their differences. Compare these animals' appearance, movements, homes, and unique characteristics.

ASSESS

Lesson Assessment: Cnidarians *(Online)*

You will complete an online assessment covering the main objectives of this lesson. Your assessment will be scored by the computer.

LEARN

Activity 3: Optional: Search for Cnidarians *(Online)*

Search the waters of the deep to explore the diverse world of cnidarians.

Safety

As always, you may wish to preview any websites before your student views them.

Name _____   Date _____

Cnidarians

Cnidarian Descriptions

Complete the missing parts.

1. Sea Anemone

How It Looks:

_____

How It Moves:

It waves from the ocean floor.

Where It Lives:

_____

Something That Makes It Unique:

_____

_____

_____

2. Jellyfish

How It Looks:

Some look like umbrellas, and some look like lion manes.

How It Moves:

_____

Where It Lives:

_____

Something That Makes It Unique:

_____

_____

_____

3. **Hydra**

   How It Looks:

   _____

   How It Moves:

   _____

   Where It Lives:

   in fresh water

   Something That Makes It Unique:

   _____

   _____

   _____

4. **Stony Coral**

   How It Looks:

   _____

   How It Moves:

   _____

   Where It Lives:

   _____

   Something That Makes It Unique:

   New corals grow on top of old ones.

Student Guide

The Diverse World of Worms

What comes to your mind when you think of worms? Soil? Slimy? There are more types of worms than the common earthworm most people think of. Look deep into the diverse world of worms. You'll be surprised at how many different kinds of worms there are in the soil, in the oceans, and in freshwater!

Lesson Objectives

- Compare segmented worms to roundworms and flatworms.
- Identify a characteristic of segmented worms (their body is made up of many ring-like segments).
- Identify characteristics of flatworms (they have eyespots and the ability to regenerate when damaged).
- Identify characteristics of roundworms (they bend from side to side to move, have nostrils but no eyes).
- State that the term *worm* is used for animals in three different phyla.

PREPARE

Approximate lesson time is 60 minutes.

Materials

For the Student

> *Come Learn with Me: Animals Without Backbones: Invertebrates* by Bridget Anderson
> ⁌Characteristics of Worms Chart

Keywords and Pronunciation

Annelida (A-nluh-duh): The phylum of invertebrate animals that includes earthworms and all other segmented worms. Earthworms, bristle worms, and leeches are part of the phylum Annelida.

cuticle: The protective layer of skin on worms. The muscles of a roundworm are covered with a skin that produces a tough layer called the cuticle.

ganglion (GANG-glee-uh): A simple, brain-like organ in some animals. In a flatworm, the eyespots are connected to the ganglia, which process information from the eyespots.

Nematoda (NEH-muh-toh-duh): The phylum of invertebrate animals that includes roundworms. Nematoda live wherever there is water.

planarian (pluh-NAIR-ee-uhn): A nonparasitic flatworm that lives in freshwater. A planarian, a type of flatworm, can regenerate its body even when it has been cut into many pieces.

Platyhelminthes: The phylum of invertebrate animals that includes more than 20,000 species of flatworms. Platyhelminthes means flat worm in Greek.

LEARN

Activity 1: Let's Read! *(Online)*

Unlike cnidarians, worms have heads and tails. Worms live in many settings, from gardens to inside animals and people. Learn about three more phyla: Platyhelminthes, Nematoda, and Annelida.

Activity 2: Characteristics of Worms *(Offline)*

Are all worms the same? Do worms that live in the soil have anything in common with worms that live in coral reefs? Use a chart to find out how the three worm phyla are related.

ASSESS

Lesson Assessment: The Diverse World of Worms *(Online)*

You will complete an online assessment covering the main objectives of this lesson. Your assessment will be scored by the computer.

LEARN

Activity 3: Optional: A Visit to Worm World *(Online)*

Did you know earthworms have five hearts? Why is a worm considered a recycler? Dig deep into this site for more information about the world of worms.

Safety

As always, you may wish to preview any websites before your student views them.

Name _____   Date _____

The Diverse World of Worms
Characteristics of Worms Chart

The worms listed below belong to different phyla, so they have similarities as well as differences. Use pages 24 to 29 of the text to find the specific characteristics of each type of worm. Look at the characteristics listed below, then decide which characteristics apply to each worm. Write "yes" in the chart if the worm has the characteristic; write "no" if it does not. Three have been completed for you.

Characteristics	Roundworms	Flatworms	Segmented Worms
Eyespots connected to ganglia			
Able to regenerate if their body is damaged			Some do
Long, slender, round bodies			
Flat bodies			
Segmented bodies			
Nostrils			
Head and tail			
Bend from side to side in order to move		Yes	No

Use the information in the chart to compare segmented worms to roundworms and flatworms.

_____

_____

_____

_____

_____

_____

Student Guide

Mighty Mollusks

We are all familiar with snails and slugs—they are mollusks. But an octopus is a mollusk too, and it seems quite different from a slug. Add to these animals the squid that moves through water, leaving an inky blackness, and you have a very diverse group of animals. What characteristics do these soft-bodied and often hard-shelled animals have in common?

Lesson Objectives

- Identify characteristics of clams, mussels, and oysters (they have two shells joined by a hinge, a siphon, and a foot for movement).
- Identify characteristics of mollusks (they have a soft body, a thick skin called a mantle, and a foot for movement).
- Identify characteristics of octopuses and squids (they have a large brain, highly developed eyes, and long arm-like appendages).
- Identify characteristics of snails and slugs (they have stalked eyes, antennae, radula, and a foot on the underside of the belly for movement).
- Identify three ways mollusks can move (using a foot extended from their body, filling their shell with air to float away, pulling with their arms, or taking water in and pushing it out of the siphon).

PREPARE

Approximate lesson time is 60 minutes.

Materials

For the Student

> *Come Learn with Me: Animals Without Backbones: Invertebrates* by Bridget Anderson
> Mollusca Crossword Puzzle

Keywords and Pronunciation

bivalve: A mollusk that has two shells connected by a hinge. Clams have two shells connected by a hinge, so they are bivalves.

cephalopod (SEH-fuh-luh-pahd): A mollusk that can swim and has appendages on its head. An octopus can swim and has tentacles, so it is a cephalopod.

gastropod (GAS-truh-pahd): A mollusk that has a foot attached to its underbelly. Most gastropods, including snails, have a single spiral shell. Slugs have no shell at all.

mantle: A thick outer covering on a mollusk's body. In some mollusks, the mantle produces a shell.

Mollusca (muh-LUH-skuh): The phylum of invertebrate animals that have a soft body, a muscular foot for movement, and a mantle. The oyster belongs to the phylum Mollusca.

radula (RA-juh-luh): The tongue-like structure of many mollusks that is covered in a hard, tooth-like substance. When a mollusk feeds, its radula can remove algae from rocks.

siphon (SIY-fuhn): In a bivalve, a tube used for breathing and feeding. A bivalve breathes and gets food by filtering the water that comes in through the siphon.

LEARN

Activity 1: Let's Read! *(Online)*

Oysters and clams actually have a soft body. A hard shell protects this vulnerable body. Learn what oysters and clams have in common with the snail, squid, octopus, and other sea animals.

Activity 2: Mollusca Puzzle *(Offline)*

Now that you know so many facts about mollusks, it's time to show off your knowledge. The Mollusca Crossword Puzzle will help you to do this. Use your book to help you find the answers.

ASSESS

Lesson Assessment: Mighty Mollusks *(Online)*

You will complete an online assessment covering the main objectives of this lesson. Your assessment will be scored by the computer.

Name _____   Date _____

The Diverse World of Worms
Mollusca Crossword Puzzle

Use the clues on the next page to complete the puzzle.

ACROSS

1. This word means "two shells."

2. It has two shells and produces pearls. It also has a siphon.

5. This gastropod has to move its foot and head out of its shell to move.

6. Its shell is lighter than those of other mollusks.

7. Snails and slugs are part of this mollusk group.

9. This bivalve can breathe under mud.

13. This cephalopod hides from enemies by squeezing into tiny places. It has a highly developed brain.

14. Cephalopods such as squid _____ by taking water into their bodies and pushing it out through their siphons.

15. A gastropod's eyes are mounted at the end of these.

16. This word means "head foot.'

DOWN

3. This is the "tongue" of a gastropod.

4. This connects the halves of a bivalve.

8. This shy cephalopod moves quickly and has very good eyesight.

10. This type of slug can grow more than 15 cm long.

11. This phylum is Latin for "soft one." Members of this phylum have soft bodies and a mantle.

12. Created by a snail's foot, this helps the snail glide over flat surfaces.

Student Guide
Arthropods

A spider crawls up a waterspout as a bee moves gracefully around a flower. In the earth a millipede moves through the loose litter of fallen leaves. In a nearby creek, a crayfish grasps at a meal with its claws. What do all these animals have in common? They are *arthropods,* animals with a segmented body and jointed legs.

Lesson Objectives

- Identify characteristics of crustaceans (they have five pairs of jointed legs, two pairs of antenna, and an exoskeleton).
- Identify characteristics of insects (they have three pairs of legs, three body segments—head, thorax, and abdomen—and one or two pairs of wings).
- Identify common characteristics of arthropods (they have jointed legs, a segmented body, and an exoskeleton).

PREPARE

Approximate lesson time is 60 minutes.

Materials

For the Student

Come Learn with Me: Animals Without Backbones: Invertebrates by Bridget Anderson
Arthropods

Keywords and Pronunciation

abdomen (AB-duh-muhn)**:** The rear body section of an arthropod. The abdomen is the back end of an insect.

Arthropoda (AHR-thruh-pah-duh)**:** The phylum of invertebrates, including insects and spiders, that have an exoskeleton, jointed legs, and a segmented body. You can easily recognize arthropods by their hard, outer covering, known as the exoskeleton, and by their jointed legs.

cephalothorax (seh-fuh-luh-THOR-aks)**:** In arachnids, the front section of the body that includes the head. An arachnid's antennae are on the cephalothorax.

chiton (KIY-tuhn)

crustacean (crustacea) (kruhs-TAY-shuhn)

entomologist (en-tuh-MAH-luh-jist)

exoskeleton (EK-soh-skeh-luh-tuhn)**:** The hard, outside body covering of an arthropod. The exoskeleton of the crab protects the animal from predators.

head: The top or front part of the body. All insects have three body parts: the head, the thorax, and the abdomen.

metamorphosis (meh-tuh-MOR-fuh-suhs)**:** The series of changes in body shape that certain animals go through as they develop from eggs to adults. The metamorphosis of a frog is from egg to tadpole to adult frog.

spinneret: An organ in some invertebrates, including spiders, that produces silk. The spinneret releases a liquid silk that the spider uses to weave a web.

thorax (THOR-aks)**:** The middle body section of many arthropods. The thorax of an arthropod lies between the head and the abdomen.

LEARN

Activity 1: Let's Read! *(Online)*

Like mollusks, arthropods are protected by an outside skeleton. Unlike mollusks, however, arthropods have a segmented body. Discover the characteristics of the phylum Arthropoda.

Activity 2: What Makes Me an Arthropod? *(Offline)*

Crustaceans and insects are part of the phylum Arthropoda. Discover some similarities and differences between these two invertebrate groups.

The phylum *Arthropoda* is made up of a very diverse group of invertebrates. Can you name some? [1]

Let' look at two smaller groups within the phylum Arthropoda. Smaller groups that make up a phylum are called *classes*. The first is the class of arthropods known as *insects*. Crustaceans, such as lobsters, make up another class. Look carefully back through the reading to compare crustaceans and insects. The Arthropods sheet will guide you to look for important information.

Answer:

1. Answers will vary but may include these: tarantulas, butterflies, hermit crabs, and centipedes.

ASSESS

Lesson Assessment: Arthropods *(Online)*

You will complete an offline assessment covering the main objectives of this unit. Your assessment will be scored by the computer.

LEARN

Activity 3: Optional: A Visit to the Museum *(Online)*

What does an entomologist study? Insects! Pick up the hand lens of an entomologist and get an up-close look at several insects, as well as other arthropods.

Safety

As always, you may wish to preview recommended websites before having your student view them.

Name _____   Date _____

Arthropods

1. Arthropods have three common characteristics. What are they?

   A. _____

   B. _____

   C. _____

2. Insects and crustaceans are two classes of arthropods. Fill in the chart to find out the characteristics that make each class unique.

Characteristics	Insects	Crustaceans
How many pairs of jointed legs do they have?		
Their bodies are divided into what parts?		fused head and thorax, abdomen
Do some have wings?		
Do they have an exoskeleton?		
Do they have antennae?		yes

3. Label the body parts of the praying mantis and lobster.

Student Guide

Echinoderms

What do sea stars, sea urchins, sand dollars, and sea cucumbers all have in common? They are all part of the phylum Echinodermata, meaning *spiny skin* in Greek. Take a closer look at these echinoderms and their common characteristics.

Lesson Objectives

- Identify characteristics of echinoderms (they are protected by hard plates, their body has radial symmetry, and they move by pumping water into their tube feet).
- Identify characteristics of sea stars (they live only in water, they have suction cups on their tube feet, their body has radial symmetry, and they are able to regenerate their body when it is damaged).

PREPARE

Approximate lesson time is 60 minutes.

Materials

For the Student

> *Come Learn with Me: Animals Without Backbones: Invertebrates* by Bridget Anderson
> Sea Stars

Keywords and Pronunciation

cephalothorax (seh-fuh-luh-THOR-aks): In arachnids, the front section of the body that includes the head. An arachnid's antennae are on the cephalothorax.

crustacean (crustacea) (kruhs-TAY-shuhn)

echinoderm (ih-KIY-nuh-durm)

Echinodermata (ih-kiy-nuh-dur-MAH-tuh): The phylum of aquatic invertebrates that are protected by a thick, spiny skin. Sea stars, sea urchins, and sand dollars are part of the phylum Echinodermata.

madreporite (MA-druh-por-iyt): A small, circular plate that filters out debris. Water enters the madreporite on the top side of a sea star's central body and is pumped to the many feet on the bottom.

LEARN

Activity 1: Let's Read! *(Online)*

Sand dollars are not really money, though they look a lot like coins. They belong to the phylum Echinodermata, which means they have thick, spiny skin covered with plates. Like sea stars, their body is symmetrical around a central point. Learn about this phylum.

Activity 2: Sea Stars *(Online)*

Sea stars are quite unusual creatures. How do they move? How do they eat? Explore and find out!

Safety

As always, you may wish to preview any websites before your student views them.

ASSESS

Lesson Assessment: Echinoderms *(Online)*

You will complete an online assessment covering the main objectives of this lesson. Your assessment will be scored by the computer.

LEARN

Activity 3: Optional: A Closer Look into the Ocean *(Online)*

There are many different types of echinoderms that live deep in the world's oceans. Visit a gallery of photographs to take a look deep into the world of echinoderms.

Safety

As always, you may wish to preview recommended websites before your student views them.

Name _____ Date _____

Echinoderms

Sea Stars

Review the Reading

Use the questions below to guide you as you re-read pages 44 to 45.

1. In what environment would you find a sea star?

_____

_____

_____

2. What happened when fishermen found a sea star, chopped it up, and threw it back into the ocean?

_____

_____

_____

3. The body of a sea star has radial symmetry. What does this mean?

_____

_____

_____

4. Why is the sea star able to stay anchored on a rock, a coral, or the bottom of the ocean?

_____

_____

_____

How a Sea Star Moves

On the website, view the movie clip titled "Sea Star Feeding." Then describe in your own words how a sea star moves. Refer to the reading as well as the text on the web page for help.

_____

_____

_____

_____

Student Guide

Classification of Invertebrates: Unit Review and Assessment

What have you learned about invertebrates? Play a game and review all you know about this diverse world of organisms!

Lesson Objectives

- Identify different groups of invertebrates (sponges, cnidarians, worms, mollusks, arthropods, echinoderms) according to their common characteristics.

PREPARE

Approximate lesson time is 60 minutes.

Materials

For the Student

Classification of Invertebrates Review Cards
Come Learn with Me: Animals Without Backbones: Invertebrates by Bridget Anderson

LEARN

Activity 1: Review the Reading *(Offline)*

Instructions

Take a moment to look back through the book. Look at the pictures. Can you identify the animals pictured and the phylum they are part of? Review the glossary for words you learned during the unit.

Now use your knowledge of invertebrates to answer each clue on the cards. Write your answer on the blank line at the bottom of each card. After you have answered all of the questions, check your answers. Correct any errors you may have made.

Now play a game with the cards. Cut out the cards, then cut each card in half on the dotted line. Turn the cards face down and arrange them in a square of eight rows and eight columns. Turn one card over and read it to yourself. Then turn another card over. Do they match? You are looking for a question and its answer. If they are not a match, turn them back over and repeat with two new cards. Pay close attention to where you place the cards—it may help you make a match!

The game is over when you have matched all the cards.

Activity 2: Invertebrate Organisms *(Online)*

What do you remember about the many invertebrates and their groups? Test your recall and observe some fantastic marine invertebrates on this website!

Safety

As always, you may wish to preview any websites before your student views them.

ASSESS

Unit Assessment: Classification of Invertebrates *(Online)*

You will complete an online assessment of the main objectives in this unit. Follow the instructions online. Your assessment will be scored by the computer.

LEARN

Activity 3: Optional: ZlugQuest Measurement *(Online)*

Name _____   Date _____

Classification of Invertebrates:
Unit Review and Assessment
Classification of Invertebrates Review Cards

I am an echinoderm. My body has radial symmetry. In order to move, I pump water into my tube feet. What is on the outside of my body? Answer: _____	You can find me only in the water. I have nostrils but no eyes. I move through the water by bending my body from side to side. What am I? Answer: _____
I am a segmented worm. What makes me different from other worms? Answer: _____	If you look at me, you'll see that my body is divided into segments with jointed legs. My body is protected by an exoskeleton. What am I? Answer: _____
I have a soft body with a thick skin called a mantle covering me. I also have a foot for movement. What am I? Answer: _____	I have tentacles coming from my body, and they have long, stinging cells on the end. What am I? Answer: _____
I am a type of worm that can regenerate a damaged body part when it is injured. I also have eyespots. What am I? Answer: _____	I am a sponge living deep in the ocean. I reproduce through budding. What else is common among sponges? Answer: _____

Student Guide

Mixtures and Solutions

Did you know that when you drink a glass of juice, iced tea, or soda, you are drinking a *solution?* Solutions are all around us. Find out how to make solutions, separate them, and how temperature affects them. Learn what the label on a juice box means when it says the drink contains 10 percent juice.

A solution is a special kind of mixture. All mixtures have parts that are mixed and mixtures have parts that do not change chemically when they are combined. But not all mixtures are solutions. Make your own mixtures and see if you can solve the mystery of which one is a solution.

Lesson Objectives

- Define a *solution* as a mixture in which the substances are completely and evenly mixed down to their individual molecules.
- Define a *substance* as anything that contains only one kind of molecule.
- Describe a *mixture* as a combination of two or more substances that maintain their individual properties and do not go through a chemical change when mixed.
- Recognize that solutions can be made from combinations of gases, liquids, and solids.

PREPARE

Approximate lesson time is 60 minutes.

Materials

For the Student

    What's the Solution?
    cup, plastic - 8 oz.
    measuring spoon - tablespoon
    powdered drink mix - one teaspoon
    sand - one teaspoon
    sugar - one teaspoon
    measuring cup
    oil, cooking - one teaspoon
    pencil
    spoon
    water

Keywords and Pronunciation

dissolve: To mix completely at the molecular level with another substance. Salt and sugar will completely dissolve in water.

mixture: A combination of two or more substances that do not change chemically when mixed. Trail mix is an example of a mixture.

solution: A mixture in which the substances are completely and evenly mixed, down to their individual molecules. Sugar-water is a solution.

substance: Anything that contains only one type of molecule. Gold is an example of a substance.

LEARN

Activity 1: Mixtures and Solutions *(Online)*

Activity 2: A Special Kind of Mixture *(Offline)*

You know that a solution is a mixture, but which mixtures are solutions? Can you find the answer? Brew up some mixtures and figure out which is which!

ASSESS

Lesson Assessment: Mixtures and Solutions *(Offline)*

You will complete an offline assessment covering the main objectives of this lesson. Your learning coach will score this assessment.

Name _____   Date _____

Mixtures and Solutions

What's the Solution?

Solutions are mixtures in which one substance completely mixes, or dissolves, into another substance. In this investigation, you will mix water with four substances: sand, sugar, powdered drink mix, and cooking oil. Your experiment will answer this research question: Which substance, when mixed with water, will completely dissolve and make a solution?

Hypothesis: Write your hypothesis below. Tell which substances you predict will dissolve in water to make a solution and which substances will not. Write complete sentences.

_____

_____

_____

_____

Materials

Water

Pencil

Sugar, 1 teaspoon 5mL - (1 teaspoon)

Measuring cup

Cooking oil, 1 teaspoon 5mL - (1 teaspoon)

Plastic cup, 8 oz., 4

Powdered drink mix, 5mL - (1 teaspoon)

Spoon

Sand, 5mL - (1 teaspoon)

Procedure

1. Fill a cup a little over halfway with water.

2. Add one 5mL of sand.

3. Stir for one minute.

4. Allow the mixture to settle.

5. Repeat steps 1 to 4 for the sugar, powdered drink mix, and cooking oil.

6. Draw how the mixtures look in the correct cups on the next page.

Scientist Notebook

1. Remember that a *variable* in an investigation is something that is changed to see how it affects something else. What is the variable?

_____

2. What effect will the variable have?

_____

_____

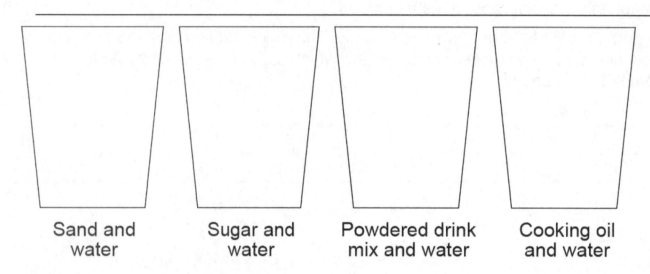

| Sand and water | Sugar and water | Powdered drink mix and water | Cooking oil and water |

Analysis

3. Which substances dissolved completely in water? How can you tell?

_____

_____

_____

4. Which substances did not dissolve completely in water? How can you tell?

_____

_____

_____

Conclusion

5. Look back at your research question. Answer it here: Which substance, when mixed with water, will completely dissolve and make a solution? Tell what you observed.

   _____

   _____

   _____

6. Look back at your hypothesis. Were your predictions correct? _____

7. After an investigation, you might have ideas for a new experiment. What other substances would you mix with water to find out if they dissolve?

   _____

   _____

   _____

Student Guide
What's Dissolving? Solvents and Solutes

Learn more words in the language of solutions, such as solute, a substance that dissolves in a solution, and *solvent,* the substance that does the dissolving. Find out what scientists call the *universal solvent.* Then, try to dissolve substances in a variety of solvents.

Lesson Objectives

- Define a *solute* as the substance that dissolves in a solution.
- Define a *solvent* as the substance that dissolves a solute to make a solution.
- Identify solute and solvents in different solutions.

PREPARE

Approximate lesson time is 60 minutes.

Materials

For the Student

> Lab Guidelines
> Solvent and Solute Mix-Up
> baking soda - 5 mL (1 teaspoon)
> cup, plastic - 8 oz (12)
> measuring spoon
> salt - 5 mL (1 teaspoon)
> soap, liquid - 10 mL (2 teaspoons)
> sugar - 5 mL (teaspoon)
> vinegar - 240 mL (1 cup)
> bowl
> graduated cylinder
> markers - permanent
> oil, cooking - 240 mL (1 cup)
> rubbing alcohol - 240 mL (1 cup)
> spoon
> water - 240 mL (1 cup)

Keywords and Pronunciation

acetic (uh-SEE-tihk)

acetone (A-suh-tohn)

colloid (KAH-loyd)

solute (SAHL-yoot) : A substance that dissolves in another substance to make a solution. Salt is the solute in saltwater.

solvent: A substance that can dissolve other substances. Water is a solvent of sugar.

LEARN

Activity 1: The "Stuff" of Solutions *(Online)*

Activity 2: Solvents and Solutes Mix-Up *(Offline)*

Water dissolves so many substances that it is often called the *universal solvent.* Will solutes dissolve in solvents other than water? Make a combination of solutions to find out.

Safety

Have your student wear safety goggles while doing this activity. Caution your student never to taste or inhale anything that is part of a Science lesson unless you have told him it is safe to do so. Do not have him taste or inhale any of the solvents.

ASSESS

Lesson Assessment: What's Dissolving? Solvents and Solutes *(Offline)*

You will complete an offline assessment covering the main objectives of this lesson. Your learning coach will score this assessment.

What's Dissolving? Solvents and Solutes

Lab Guidelines

Our goal is to provide you with as many effective, rich laboratory experiences as possible. Sometimes this means that virtual options and field options are part of our courses, allowing you to use apparatuses that are too expensive or dangerous, or getting you to focus on the environment near you.

Labs where the materials are not in front of you require a different approach than more traditional lab activities. Sometimes these may be truly virtual labs, while others, they may be field studies that require a computer to analyze data. In all cases, when you do a lab, think about the various settings that the lab might be done in and ask yourself if you feel that you could complete the lab in that setting. For example, if you are using a virtual microscope, be sure that you are also thinking about how a real microscope would look, feel and work.

Virtual experiences will not be exactly like real experiences in the lab. Pay strict attention to the safety considerations that you would think about if it were a real lab. When doing field studies, carefully inventory the dangers in your local environment that may be dangerous animals and plants, bad weather or other dangers that are a natural part of the area you are studying.

We have worked hard to see to it that virtual DATA is as much like real data as possible. This means that the data that you acquire in most cases will not be the same as someone elses, and will be subject to the uncertainty and error that you would find in a similar real life lab.

Work hard on these experiences keeping these ideas in mind. You never know when you might be doing this lab or field study in a different setting!

Safety in the Lab

Scientists understand that conducting experiments involves a certain amount of hazard and risk. They have identified certain safety practices and guidelines that address the hazards and risks involved in laboratory work. Follow these practices and guidelines and use common sense to ensure your safety in the laboratory.

Lab Setup

- Make sure your lab area has adequate ventilation. When possible, open windows; otherwise, turn the fan switch on your thermostat to the ON position. Set up an electric fan to help ventilate the lab area.
- Keep drawers and cabinets closed to prevent physical hazards.
- Identify a location with easy and immediate access to fresh, running water. This is important for flushing eyes and skin in case of contact with chemicals.
- If you are using an area where food is prepared or consumed, secure all food items in such a way as to avoid contamination.
- Keep a fire extinguisher in the lab area and know how to use it.
- Post the number to the nearest poison control center near a telephone. You can find this number by calling the national poison control number: **1-800-222-1222.**

Personal Protection

- Wear gloves throughout lab preparation, the entire lab procedure, and during cleanup when working with chemicals. Always dispose of the used gloves before leaving the lab area.
- Wear clothing you can remove easily in case of an accident. Clothes should cover the body from the neck to at least the knees.
- Wear closed-toe and closed-heel shoes. Do not wear high heels, shoes made of woven materials, or sandals in the lab area.
- Tie back long hair and remove jewelry before entering the lab area.

Lab Protocol

- If possible, have an adult or peer present while conducting all labs.
- Never ingest anything in the lab. Eating, drinking, and chewing gum are not allowed.
- Do not ingest, taste, or smell any chemicals.
- Flames are not allowed in the lab area when using flammable gas or liquids.
- Keep chemical and solution containers closed until they are needed.
- Assemble laboratory apparatus away from the edge of working surfaces.
- Never pipet by mouth.
- Do not shake filled test tubes or beakers, unless directed to do so in the lab procedure.
- Never place materials on the floor, unless directed to do so in the lab procedure.
- Never leave an experiment unattended, unless directed to do so in the lab procedure.
- Always check glassware, and discard any with chips, breaks, or cracks in a safe manner.
- Clean up broken glassware as soon as it is safe to do so, and discard in a safe manner.
- Clean glassware before returning it to storage.
- Always wash your hands thoroughly with soap and water after cleanup and before eating or drinking.
- Clean up spills immediately.
- Always discard used and spilled chemicals and solutions down the drain, diluted with plenty of water.

General Procedures

Follow these general procedures each time you conduct an experiment. They will help you develop good lab practices.

Setting Up and Maintaining Your Lab Area

- Read through the entire procedure before beginning any lab.

- Review the list of materials prior to any lab because you may need to supply several items. Gather all materials in your lab area before beginning any lab.
- Set up a lab area where you can organize your materials and have room to set up your lab. (For most labs, a countertop or table will work well.)
- Always keep a copy of the Laboratory Guidelines in your lab area. Follow all procedures in the Lab Setup section of these guidelines.
- When using measuring utensils in several steps, wash and dry the utensils between steps.
- If you do not complete a lab, store all materials out of the reach of small children or pets until you are ready to complete the lab. Notify everyone in the home that you are conducting an experiment, and tell them not to touch it.

Cleaning Up Your Lab Area

- Clean up and properly store materials after each lab. (Materials and equipment are reused in labs.)
- Thoroughly clean your hands, as well as surfaces, containers, and like items, with soap and water. Thoroughly dry materials before storing them.

Taking Good Measurements

Take careful measurements during a lab, and repeat tests until you are confident about your results. If you think there is an error (for example, if you are not certain that you started the stopwatch at the right time or you think you miscounted the time), do the procedure again.

- Length: Measure in centimeters (cm) or tenths of a centimeter, depending on the detail you are able to observe.
- Time: Measure in seconds (s) or minutes (min).
- Temperature: Measure in degrees Celsius (°C).
- Volume: Measure in milliliters (mL).
- Mass: Measure in grams (g).

Recording Data

Use a data table to record your data. Make sure your data tables are prepared before you do the lab. You may use scratch paper to record your data during the lab, and then transfer your data to a computer for a final report.

Plotting Data

Plot the independent variable on the x-axis (horizontal) and the dependent variable on the y-axis (vertical).

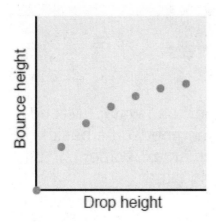

Drawing Trend Lines

Use trend lines to show the general relationship between the independent and dependent variables. Trend lines may be straight or show a curve, but they are not an attempt to connect every point on a graph.

Connecting Points (Incorrect)

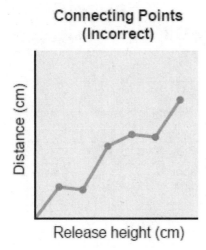

Trend Line (Correct)

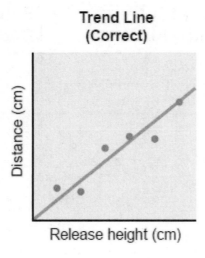

Trend Line (Correct)

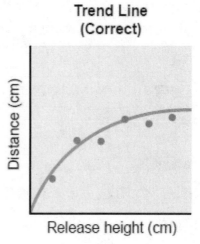

Name _____   Date _____

What's Dissolving? Solvents and Solutes
Solvent and Solute Mix-up

Will solutes that dissolve in water dissolve in solvents other than water? Mix up some different solutions to find out. Before you begin, remember some basic experiment rules: **NEVER** taste anything you are testing in an experiment. In this activity, it's a good idea not to smell anything you're testing either.

Hypothesis

Predict which solutes will dissolve in each solvent by writing yes or no in the chart. For example, if you think that salt will dissolve in alcohol, write yes in the box under Alcohol, in the row labeled Salt.

Solutes	Solvent – Soapy Water	Solvent - Alcohol	Solvent – Cooling Oil	Solvent - Vinegar
Salt				
Sugar				
Baking Soda				

Materials

salt – 15 mL (1 teaspoon)

graduated cylinder

sugar – 15 mL (1 teaspoon)

measuring spoons

baking soda – 15 mL (1 teaspoon)

cups, plastic – 8 oz – 12

soap – 10 mL (2 teaspoons)

bowl

water – 240 mL (1 cup)

marker

alcohol – 240 mL (1 cup)

spoon

cooking oil – 240 mL (1 cup)

vinegar – 240 mL (1 cup)

Procedure

1. Use a marker to label your cups. Remember, when naming solutions, the solute comes first. For example, the first cup should be labeled "Salt/Soapy Water." There should be three cups each of soapy water, alcohol, cooking oil, and vinegar and their various solutes.

2. In a bowl, mix the soap with 150 mL of water to make soapy water.

3. Use the cylinder to fill each cup with 50 mL of each solvent. Rinse the graduated cylinder before measuring the different types of solvents.

4. In the cup labeled "Salt/Soapy Water," add 5 mL (1 teaspoon) of salt to the soapy water. Stir for one minute.

5. Let the mixture settle then observe. Record in the data chart whether or not the solute was dissolved in the solvent.

6. Rinse the spoon, and then repeat adding 5 mL (1 teaspoon) salt to each solvent in the order shown on the chart. Record your observations.

7. Repeat steps 4 to 6 for the sugar and baking soda.

Observations

Solutes	Solvent – Soapy Water	Solvent - Alcohol	Solvent – Cooling Oil	Solvent - Vinegar
Salt				
Sugar				
Baking Soda				

Scientist Notebook

Think back to the research question at the top of the page. You are testing whether or not solutes that dissolve in water (salt, sugar, and baking soda) will dissolve in substances other than water.

Remember that a *variable* is something that is changed in an experiment to see how it affects something else. In this experiment, for each solvent, what is the variable?

_____

_____

_____

Analysis

Which mixtures appear to have a completely dissolved solute? (Remember to write the name of the solute first)

_____

_____

Which mixtures appear to have solute that is not completely dissolved? (Remember to write the name of the solute first).

_____

_____

Conclusion

Compare your hypothesis table to your observations and results. Which predictions were correct?

_____

_____

How can you tell if a solute dissolves into a solvent?

_____

_____

To Impress Your Friends

When you mixed the baking soda and vinegar, you might have noticed some fizzing and noise. This mixture is actually **NOT** a solution! The fizzing means that there was gas being released as the result of a chemical reaction. Sodium bicarbonate reacted with the acid in the vinegar to form carbon dioxide gas.

Student Guide
Separating Solutions

Now that you have learned how to make solutions, find out how to separate them. Separating solutions can be harder than you think. You can separate simple mixtures by hand or with a filter. Discover three different ways to separate solutions.

Lesson Objectives

- Describe ways to separate solutions, such as evaporation, chromatography, and distillation.

PREPARE

Approximate lesson time is 60 minutes.

Advance Preparation

- You will need colored candy-coated chocolate for this activity.

Materials

For the Student

Evaporation and Distillation
cup, plastic - 8 oz.
household item - pot holder
pot with lid
sugar - 60 mL (1/4 cup)
bowl
heat source
spoon
water - 240 mL (1 cup)
The Makeup of Markers
cup, plastic (4)
household item - coffee filters (4)
marker, black water soluble - blue, green and brown
pencil
rubbing alcohol
ruler, metric
scissors
jar - 1 gallon wide-mouth
water - preferably distilled
Candy Chromatography
coffee filter (4)
food - 4 colors of colored candy
food - candy-coated candy

salt - (1 gram or approximately 1/6 teaspoon)
markers - black
toothpicks
water - (1 liter or approximately 4.25 cups)

Keywords and Pronunciation

centrifuge (SEN-trih-fyooj)

chromatography (kroh-muh-TAH-gruh-fee)

desalination (dee-sa-lih-NAY-shuhn)

distillation: A way of separating liquid substances in a solution that involves heating a liquid and condensing the vapors or gases that form. We used distillation to purify the water.

evaporation: A way of separating substances in a solution that involves heating a liquid to a gas then collecting the leftover solute. Evaporation takes place when you heat water to the boiling point.

paper chromatography: A way of identifying the components of a mixture by treating them with a solvent then observing how they travel on absorbent paper. When you use black ink in paper chromatography, a rainbow of colors will travel up the paper.

solute (SAHL-yoot)**:** A substance that dissolves in another substance to make a solution. Salt is the solute in saltwater.

LEARN

Activity 1: Let's Separate Solutions *(Online)*

Safety

Caution your student not to try the distillation process on ethanol and water. This is a very dangerous procedure that only scientists should perform in their laboratory.

Activity 2: Evaporation and Distillation *(Offline)*

Separate a solution of sugar and water by evaporation and distillation.

Safety

Use extreme caution when working with boiling water. Never leave your student unattended near hot or boiling water.

Activity 3: The Makeup of Markers *(Offline)*

Complete this sentence: yellow and blue make _____. Red and blue make _____. But what colors make up brown? Explore the ink solutions used to make up marker colors to find out.

ASSESS

Lesson Assessment: Separating Solutions *(Offline)*

You will complete an offline assessment covering the main objectives of this lesson. Your learning coach will score this assessment.

LEARN

Activity 4: Optional: Pollution Solution *(Offline)*

Find out about pollution in your air by separating particles from the air.

Set jars filled with about 1 inch of distilled water in different locations outside. Leave the jars outside uncovered for 30 days. Then, bring the jars in and heat the water to evaporate the remaining water. You'll see different particles that were once in the air!

Compare the samples to determine which area had the most polluted air.

Activity 5: Optional: Candy Chromatography *(Offline)*

Your favorite candy color is actually made from a mixture of food dyes. Use paper chromatography to find out what substances make the reds, greens, blues, and yellows of candy taste so sweet!

Name _____   Date _____

Separating Solutions
Evaporation and Distillation

Evaporation and distillation are two ways of separating solutions. The particles in solutions are too small to be separated by other means such as filtering or by hand. A more complicated process is needed to get those particles out!

Materials

sugar + water solution : 240 mL (1cup) water + (1/4 cup) sugar

spoon for stirring

pot with lid

cup, plastic, 8 oz.

bowl

pot holder

Evaporation Procedure

1. Stir the sugar and water together in the bowl thoroughly.
2. Pour 120 mL (1/2 cup) of the solution into a plastic cup.
3. Place the cup in a warm, sunny, dry place.
4. Check it every day for a week.

What do you expect to happen to the water?

_____

_____

Imagine a week has gone by. You check your cup and find no water. What else might you notice?

_____

_____

_____

How could you speed up the evaporation process?

_____

_____

_____

Distillation Procedure

1. Heat the rest of the sugar-water solution in a pot.

2. Once the water boils, place the lid on the pot to trap some of the water vapor.

3. Use a potholder to carefully lift the lid from the pot. Place it on a heat-resistant surface with the inside of the lid facing up. Let the vapor cool and condense then pour it into a cup.

Do you notice any sugar remaining in the pot? _____

What's the main difference between evaporating the solution and distilling it?

_____

_____

_____

Think of the two ways you separated the sugar from the water. Which way seems to be the best to you? Why?

_____

_____

_____

Challenge

Try to think of some real-life situations in which mixtures of substances must be separated. Think about home, business, the environment, etc. How are evaporation and distillation used in these situations? Find out about technology that makes separating solutions quick and easy.

Name   Date

Separating Solutions
The Makeup of Markers

You can use paper chromatography to study the colors of ink that make up different colored markers. By using a solvent and a special paper that will soak up color, you can see what inks make up certain colors.

Materials

markers- black, blue, green, brown

coffee filters – 4

cups, plastic- 4

water

scissors

pencil

rubbing alcohol

ruler

Procedure

1. Cut a strip about 20 cm long and 3 cm wide from each coffee filter.

2. With a pencil, mark a spot 10 cm from the bottom of the strip.

3. Start with the black marker. Make a small dot (1 cm) at the 10 cm mark on the strip.

4. Repeat steps 2 and 3 with each marker.

5. Fill the plastic cups with 5 cm of water. Add about 1 cm of rubbing alcohol. This is your solvent.

6. Place each strip of coffee filter into the cup. Do not let the marker dots contact the solvent.

7. Watch as the coffee filters absorb the solvent. Observe the marker dots.

Observations

1. What happened to the marker dots when the solvent reached them?

   _____

   _____

2. What colors did you see?

   _____

   _____

3. Which markers were made from more than one color of ink?

   _____

   _____

What Happened?

The solvent moved through the paper because of capillary action. The solvent dissolved the ink in the markers. Each color of ink traveled a different distance on the paper, depending on the attraction the ink has for the paper (a solid) or the solvent (a liquid).

Try It:

After the lesson, you may want to try the Beyond the Lesson activity to compare the dyes in colored candy-coated foods. Or, compare the same color for different brands of candies—for example four different reds or greens.

Interesting fact:

Scientists can learn a great deal from a chromatogram—for example, exactly what substances are in a certain dye and how much of each color is present. Detectives who study *forensic science* may use chromatography to study a paint sample from a car. They can find out the model of the car and the year it was made!

Name _____   Date _____

Separating Solutions
Candy Chromatography

Candy Chroma-what? "Chromo" is a Greek word for color. Because food dyes are made of different colors, you can use paper chromatography to study them. To do it, you need paper that can soak up the different colors and a solvent that will dissolve the dyes.

Materials

4 different colors of colored candy coated chocolate

salt solution (1 gram salt + 1 liter water)

filter paper or coffee filter - 4 sheets

4 plastic cups

toothpicks

metric ruler

scissors

pencil

marker, black

Take Color Samples

1. Label each cup with one color of each candy.

2. Place one candy sample in each cup.

3. Put a few drops of water (about 5) in one of the cups.

4. Use a toothpick to carefully stir the candy in the water to take off as much color as you can without disturbing the white candy coating.

5. Remove the candy as soon as you see the white candy coating.

6. Repeat for the other three samples.

Label the Paper

7. Use a pencil to label your filter paper with each color of the candy (ink may get in the way of your results).

8. Fold the filter paper in half twice, once lengthwise and then widthwise. When you unfold it you should see the lines crossing in the center.

9. Draw a circle about 2 cm across around the center of each filter paper.

10. When you add the solvent, make sure you place it within the circles.

Paper Chromatography

11. Use the toothpick to place a spot of each color sample in its labeled circle. Repeat several times to get a lot of the dye on each spot. Wait for each sample to dry.

12. Put the salt solution into a clear cup, keeping the water level below 0.5 centimeters.

13. Fold the filter paper and stand it up in the cup. Just the tip of the paper should touch the salt solution. Make sure the solution does not touch the circles you drew in pencil.

14. Watch for *capillary action* as the solvent moves up the paper, pulling the colors in the dye! This should take about 10 minutes.

15. When the solution is about 1 cm from the edge, take the paper out.

16. Each sheet of filter paper is a chromatogram. Let your chromatograms dry.

What Happened?

The salt-water solution moved through the paper because of capillary action. The salt-water solution dissolved the colors in the dye. Each color dye traveled different distances on the paper depending on the attraction it has for the paper (a solid) or the solvent (a liquid).

Think About It:

For each sample which color traveled the farthest? Which has the most colors in its dye?

Try It:

You can compare colors in other colored candy coated foods, or compare the same color for different brands of candies, for example 4 different reds or greens.

Student Guide
Dissolving Solutions Quickly

Crushing and grinding solid solutes helps to speed up the process of dissolving. Stirring and shaking also makes many solutes dissolve faster in solvents. Try crushing sugar cubes to see if you've got the power to make things dissolve—fast!

Lesson Objectives

- Describe two ways to increase the rate at which solids dissolve in liquids (by crushing them into smaller pieces and by stirring).
- Recognize that breaking up a solute into smaller pieces increases its surface area.

PREPARE

Approximate lesson time is 60 minutes.

Advance Preparation

- If you don't already have it, you will need 12 sugar cubes for this activity.

Materials

For the Student

    Grind, Shake, and Stir
    household item - container with lids (2)
    household item - large wooden spoon or similar utensil
    household item - plastic sandwich bag
    sugar cube (12)
    graduated cylinder
    paper, notebook
    spoon (2)
    timer
    water - 480 mL (2 cups)

Keywords and Pronunciation

solute (SAHL-yoot): A substance that dissolves in another substance to make a solution. Salt is the solute in saltwater.

surface area: The amount of space the outer face of an object takes up. The six surfaces of the block of wood took up 600 millimeters squared of space, so the surface area is 600 millimeters squared.

LEARN

Activity 1: Slow or Speedy? What's the Secret? *(Online)*

Activity 2: Grind, Shake, and Stir *(Offline)*

Dissolve a sugar cube whole and a ground sugar cube by shaking and stirring to see which will dissolve faster.

ASSESS

Lesson Assessment: Dissolving Solutions Quickly *(Online)*

You will complete an online assessment covering the main objectives of this lesson. Your assessment will be scored by the computer.

Name _____   Date _____

Dissolving Solutions Quickly
Grind, Shake, and Stir

A riddle:

What do a crushed sugar cube and a whole sugar cube have in common?

Answer:

Well, **EVERYTHING**! They're exactly the same, except the surface area of a crushed sugar cube is much larger than the whole one.

Surface area is an important thing to know about when studying solutions. By now, you have had quite a bit of practice making solutions. When you mixed things such as sugar and water or salt and vinegar, did the particles of solute dissolve right away? Did stirring make any difference?

Solutes will dissolve faster in a solvent if more of its surface area is exposed. For substances with larger surface areas, the solvent has more to work with while doing the dissolving.

You can do the following demonstration to see how this works.

Materials

sugar cubes (12)

plastic sandwich bag

water 480 mL (2 cups)

graduated cylinder

large wooden spoon or similar utensil

plastic container, with lid (2)

spoon (2)

timer

paper

Science notebook

Which has more surface area?

Procedure:

1. Pour 125 mL (1/2 cup) of water into each plastic container.

2. Place three sugar cubes in the plastic sandwich bag, seal it, and use the back of a large wooden spoon or similar utensil to grind them into a fine powder.

3. At exactly the same time, carefully add the three powdered cubes from the sandwich bag to one container and three whole cubes to the other container.

4. Start the timer and stir both solutions.

5. Record the time it took for the powdered sugar cubes and the whole sugar cubes to dissolve.

6. Repeat steps 1 to 5 but cover the containers with their lids and shake the solutions instead of stirring them.

Amount of time to dissolve with stirring:

whole sugar cubes _____

crushed sugar cubes _____

Amount of time to dissolve with shaking:

whole sugar cubes _____

crushed sugar cubes _____

Questions:

1. Which dissolved faster, the whole sugar cubes or the crushed sugar cubes?

_____

2. Did the results of your demonstration match what you've read and heard about surface area?

_____

_____

3. Why does shaking and stirring speed up the rate of dissolving even more?

_____

_____

_____

4. Imagine you wanted to dissolve powdered drink mix in water? How would you make this happen quickly?

_____

_____

_____

EXTENSION

Try letting the sugar dissolve on its own without shaking or stirring. How long does it take the sugar to dissolve now?

Student Guide
Solubility

Some substances are soluble meaning they will mostly dissolve in a solvent. Some are *somewhat soluble,* and only partially dissolve. Still others are just plain *insoluble* and dissolve in only very small amounts in specific solvents. Changing the temperature of the solvent can change the solubility of substances as well. Compare substances for solubility, and then observe the effects of increasing temperature while creating a saltwater and sugar-water solution.

Lesson Objectives

- Classify substances as soluble, insoluble, and somewhat soluble.
- Define *solubility* as the maximum total amount of a solid that can dissolve into a given quantity of a particular solvent at a given temperature.
- Recognize that increasing the temperature of a solvent can change the solubility of a solid solute.
- Recognize that increasing the temperature of a solvent usually increases the rate at which a solute dissolves.
- Recognize that not all substances dissolve in a given quantity of water in the same amounts.

PREPARE

Approximate lesson time is 60 minutes.

Materials

For the Student

> Is It Soluble?
> cornstarch - 10 mL (2 tsp.)
> cup, plastic - 8 oz. (6)
> measuring spoon
> sand - 10 mL (2 tsp.)
> sugar - 10 mL (2 tsp.)
> funnel
> graduated cylinder
> paper towels (3)
> spoon
> water
> How Many Spoonfuls to Saturation?
> jar - glass (4)
> pot with lid
> salt
> sugar

thermometer, Celsius/Fahrenheit
heat source
measuring cup
water - 400 mL

Keywords and Pronunciation

acetone (A-suh-tohn)

saturated: Dissolving the greatest possible amount of a substance in a solution. The liquid in a hummingbird feeder is a supersaturated solution of sugar and water.

solubility (sahl-yuh-BIH-luh-tee)**:** How much solute can be dissolved in a solvent at a given temperature. The solubility of the sugar increased when we raised the temperature.

soluble (SAHL-yuh-buhl)**:** Able to be dissolved. Sugar is soluble in water.

solute (SAHL-yoot)**:** A substance that dissolves in another substance to make a solution. Salt is the solute in saltwater.

LEARN

Activity 1: Why Doesn't It All Dissolve? *(Online)*

Activity 2: Soluble, Insoluble, and Somewhat Soluble *(Offline)*

Use a filter to find out if certain substances are soluble, insoluble, or somewhat soluble.

Activity 3: Solubility and Temperature *(Offline)*

Dissolve salt and sugar into hot and cold water to compare the effects of temperature on solubility.

Safety

Never leave your student unattended near a stove, oven, or microwave. Use extreme caution when working with boiling water. Never leave your student unattended near hot or boiling water.

ASSESS

Lesson Assessment: Solubility *(Online)*

You will complete an online assessment covering the main objectives of this lesson. Your assessment will be scored by the computer.

140

Name _____   Date _____

Solubility
Is It Soluble?

The amount of solute that can dissolve in a particular solvent is the solute's solubility. Investigate the solubility of three different substances. Which will be soluble: cornstarch, sugar, or sand?

Hypothesis:

Write a sentence predicting whether cornstarch, sugar, or sand will be soluble, insoluble, or somewhat soluble.

_____

_____

Materials:

funnel

paper towel – 3

water

cornstarch – 10 mL (2 tsp.)

sugar – 10 mL (2 tsp.)

sand – 10 mL (2 tsp.)

plastic cups, 8 oz. – 6

spoon

graduated cylinder

measuring spoon

How to Make a Filter

Procedure:

1. In a plastic cup, mix 100 mL of water with 10 mL of sugar.

2. Fold one paper towel to make a filter as shown.

3. Place the filter into a funnel.

4. Set the funnel in an empty plastic cup.

5. Hold the funnel steady as you carefully pour the mixture of water and sugar through the filter.

6. After 2 minutes, observe the solution that flows into the empty cup and the filter for signs of sugar. If the sugar were completely soluble, all of it would have passed through the filter.

7. Record your observations in the chart.

8. Repeat steps 1 to 7 for the sand and cornstarch.

Scientist Notebook:

You are testing the solubility of different substances. The variable is what you change in each test. What is your variable in this investigation?

_____

_____

_____

Observations and Results:

Mixture	Any solute on filter?	Any solute in water?
Sugar + water		
Sand + water		
Cornstarch + water		

Conclusion:

A filter will allow substances that are dissolved to pass right through. Substances that have not dissolved will be blocked.

1. Which substance was soluble that is dissolved? Which was insoluble? Which was somewhat soluble?

_____

_____

_____

2. What evidence do you have that a substance was soluble, insoluble, or somewhat soluble?

_____

_____

_____

3. Re-read your hypothesis. Was your prediction correct?

_____

_____

_____

4. How can you check the sugar + water solution that passed through the filter to be sure that the solute passed through?

_____

_____

_____

Name   Date

Solubility

How Many Spoonfuls to Saturation?

For many solid solutes, grinding and stirring are two ways to dissolve them more quickly. A third way to do this is to increase the temperature of your solvent. Try this experiment to see how this works.

Materials:

salt

sugar

water, 400 ml

heat source

glass jar – 4

spoon

thermometer

graduated cylinder

measuring cups

Procedure:

1. Pour 100 mL of hot water into one glass jar and the same amount of cold water into another.

2. Find the temperature for each cup of water. Record the temperature in the chart.

3. Stir 25 ml of sugar into each jar.

4. Continue adding sugar to each of the cups until they become saturated and no more sugar will dissolve. You may have to wait a while.

5. In the chart, record the total number of ml of sugar added to each solution.

6. Repeat steps 1 to 4 using salt instead of sugar. Re-heat the hot water to the same temperature as it was for the sugar.

Observations:

mL of solute added

Solute	Hot Temperature:	Cold Temperature:
Sugar		
Salt		

Analysis:

On the graph below, draw a dot to show how many grams of solute dissolved in each temperature of water. When you are finished, connect the dots to see a simple solubility graph. Most provided thermometers register temperatures below 70 degrees F. If yours does not you might want to consider purchasing a thermometer at a drug store or hobby store.

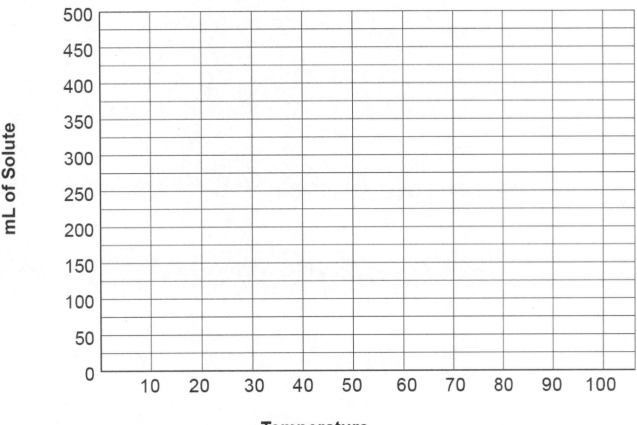

Conclusion::

1. Which substance is most soluble in water, salt or sugar?

    _____

2. Which two things determine when a solution will be saturated?

    _____

    _____

    _____

    _____

Student Guide

Concentrations

What's the difference between weak tea and strong tea? Not all cups of tea look, smell, and taste alike. They differ depending on their *concentration*—the amount of solute dissolved in them. Learn the terms *diluted* and *concentrated* and compare the difference between these types of solutions in a taste test.

Lesson Objectives

- Compare the concentrations of different solutions and describe them as concentrated or dilute.
- Recognize that, at a given temperature, a solution is saturated when the maximum amount of solute has been dissolved into the solvent.
- State the concentration of solutions as the number of grams of solute per 100 grams of solvent.

PREPARE

Approximate lesson time is 60 minutes.

Advance Preparation

- You will need to wait for a juice solution to freeze to complete this activity. You may choose to start the activity early then return to it during the lesson, or to do the activity during the lesson and return to it later. Have your student complete the Not Too Sweet: Solution Dilution lab sheet up to the Observations section, then finish the lab sheet after the solution has completely frozen.

Materials

For the Student

    Not Too Sweet: Solution Dilution
    cup, plastic - 8 oz. (6)
    freezing source
    household item - ice cube tray
    powdered drink mix - one packet
    sugar - 480 mL (2 cups)
    bowl - or pitcher
    graduated cylinder
    markers
    measuring cup
    spoon
    tape, masking
    toothpicks (6)
    water

---

food - oil-based salad dressing
juice
milk
flashlight
glass, drinking (3)

Keywords and Pronunciation

colloid (KAH-loyd)**:** a heterogeneous mixture from which the suspended particles do not settle out

concentrated: Containing a large amount of solute. The juice in the frozen section of the grocery store is very concentrated, and we have to add water before we can drink it.

concentration: The amount of one substance dissolved in another. Weak and strong tea have different concentrations.

diluted: Containing very little solute. Weak tea is a very diluted solution and contains more water than tea.

solubility (sahl-yuh-BIH-luh-tee)**:** How much solute can be dissolved in a solvent at a given temperature. The solubility of the sugar increased when we raised the temperature.

solute (SAHL-yoot)**:** A substance that dissolves in another substance to make a solution. Salt is the solute in saltwater.

LEARN

Activity 1: Concentrating on Solutions *(Online)*

Activity 2: Not Too Sweet *(Offline)*

Adding water to concentrated solutions causes them to become diluted. Observe what happens when you dilute a solution to make a tasty treat.

ASSESS

Lesson Assessment: Concentrations *(Online)*

You will complete an online assessment covering the main objectives of this lesson. Your assessment will be scored by the computer.

LEARN

Activity 3: Optional: New Mixtures: Colloids and Suspensions *(Offline)*

Solutions are not the only type of mixtures. Other mixtures have names such as *colloid, gel, aerosol, suspension,* or *emulsion.* Let's examine two of these types of mixtures—colloids and suspensions.

The difference between a solution, a colloid, and a suspension is in the size of the particles of solute.

Solutions:

- Very small particles made of individual molecules
- Particles are distributed evenly.
- Particles dissolve.
- Particles cannot be separated by a filter.
- Solutions are transparent, although they may have a color.

Colloids:

- Particles are made of clumps of molecules.
- Particles spread evenly, but do not dissolve.
- Particles stay mixed and do not settle to the bottom.
- Colloids cannot be separated by a filter.
- Colloids look murky and opaque.
- Milk, fog, and smoke are examples of colloids.
- Particles in colloids can scatter light. Think, for example, about how fog scatters a car's headlights.

Suspensions:

- They have larger particles.
- Particles are large enough to separate and settle to the bottom.
- Suspensions can be separated by a filter.
- Suspensions look murky and opaque.
- Suspensions do not transmit light.
- Oil-based salad dressings are an example of suspensions.
- If a label on something says "shake well before using", it is probably an example of a suspension.
- Blood is a suspension.

Observe the different properties of oil-and-vinegar salad dressing (suspension), milk (colloid), and juice (solution). Here are some things to try:

1. Observe the look and feel of each mixture.

2. Shake or stir each mixture and observe the separation properties.

Try something called the *Tyndall Effect.* Use a flashlight to shine a beam of light through each mixture. Observe how they transmit or scatter light.

Name _____   Date _____

Concentrations

Not Too Sweet: Solution Dilution

You've learned that concentration means the percent of solute to the amount of solvent. Store-bought juice has labels that show the percent fruit juice to the amount of water. Tears contain a certain concentration of salt to water. Concentrations of solutions are important in chemistry and medicine, too.

Here's a sweet way to investigate concentrations. By mixing powdered drink mix and sugar, you can taste the difference between solutions that are diluted and concentrated. This activity is a special exception to the "No Tasting" rule we follow during investigations. Another way to investigate concentration besides tasting is _____.

Materials:

cups - 8 oz, clear plastic (6)

water

pitcher or bowl

graduated cylinder

toothpicks (6)

powdered drink mix – 1 packet

sugar – 480 mL (2 cups)

spoon

measuring cup

masking tape

marker

ice tray

freezer

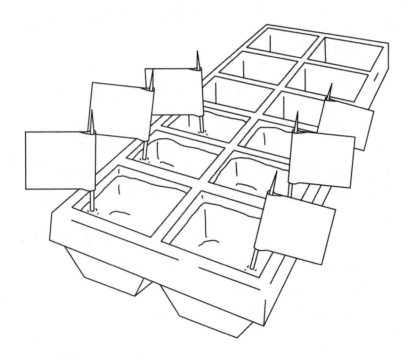

Procedure:

1. Use a marker to label the cups from 1 to 6.

2. In the pitcher or bowl, mix 2 liters of water, one packet of drink mix, and 480 mL sugar. Stir the solution until the sugar dissolves.

3. Pour 100mL of the solution into each of the six cups.

4. Add water to each cup in the following amounts and stir:

    Cup 1: none
    Cup 2: 25 mL
    Cup 3: 50 mL
    Cup 4: 75 mL
    Cup 5: 100 mL
    Cup 6: 125 mL

Do you notice a color change? _____

5. Use the tape and marker to label the toothpicks 1 to 6. Lay the toothpicks in their own spots in the ice cube tray as shown in the picture above.

6. Pour a sample from each cup into an ice cube tray according to the toothpick label. For example, pour the solution from Cup 1 into the part of the tray with the toothpick labeled 1.

7. Carefully put the tray in the freezer until the solution completely freezes.

Observations:

1. Describe the changes in the color of each ice cube.

    _____

    _____

    _____

2. What if the color of the powdered drink mix seemed to disappear? Would there still be some of the powdered drink mix in the cube? Explain.

    _____

    _____

    _____

3. Taste each cube. Describe the differences in taste.

    _____

    _____

    _____

4. Is there some sugar in all of the cups? _____

5. Could you have performed this concentration test without freezing the juice?

    _____

    _____

    _____

Student Guide

Chemistry of Solutions: Unit Review and Assessment

Now that you have mixed your last cup of sugar water and made your first diluted ice pop, it's time to review. Take a look back at all the facts you have uncovered about solutions. After your review, you will take the assessment to show what you have learned.

Lesson Objectives

- Describe ways to separate solutions, such as evaporation, chromatography, and distillation.
- Classify substances as soluble, insoluble, and somewhat soluble.
- Compare the concentrations of different solutions and describe them as concentrated or dilute.
- Define a *solute* as the substance that dissolves in a solution.
- Define a *solution* as a mixture in which the substances are completely and evenly mixed down to their individual molecules.
- Define a *solvent* as the substance that dissolves a solute to make a solution.
- Describe a *mixture* as a combination of two or more substances that maintain their individual properties and do not go through a chemical change when mixed.
- Describe two ways to increase the rate at which solids dissolve in liquids (by crushing them into smaller pieces and by stirring).
- Recognize that increasing the temperature of a solvent can change the solubility of a solid solute.
- Recognize that increasing the temperature of a solvent usually increases the rate at which a solute dissolves.
- Recognize that not all substances dissolve in a given quantity of water in the same amounts.
- Recognize that solutions can be made from combinations of gases, liquids, and solids.
- Identify solute and solvents in different solutions.

PREPARE

Approximate lesson time is 60 minutes.

Materials

For the Student

Crossword Chemistry
pencil

LEARN

Activity 1: Crossword Chemistry *(Offline)*

Complete a crossword puzzle to review what you know about solutions.

ASSESS

Unit Assessment: Chemistry of Solutions *(Offline)*

Complete an offline Unit Assessment. Your learning coach will score the assessment.

LEARN

Activity 2: Optional: ZlugQuest Measurement *(Online)*

Name _____   Date _____

Chemistry of Solutions: Unit Review and Assessment

Crossword Chemistry

Word Bank

substance	mixture	diluted
solution	evaporation	concentrated
dissolve	saturated	paper chromatography
surface area	soluble	solvent
concentration	solubility	
solute	distillation	

Across

2. A solution that contains very little solute is _____.

5. _____ is a way of identifying the substances in a mixture by treating them with a solvent, then observing how they travel on absorbent paper.

7. You can dissolve 200 grams of sugar in 100 g of water at room temperature. This statement describes sugar's _____.

8. The amount of space the outer face of an object takes up is called _____.

9. A _____ is a combination of two or more substances that do not change chemically when you mix them.

9. This bivalve can breathe under mud.

11. _____ is a way of separating liquid substances in a solution that involves heating a liquid and condensing the vapors or gasses that form.

13. To _____ means to break up and mix completely with another substance.

15. A _____ is anything that contains only one type of molecule.

Down

1. On juice labels, the amount of fruit juice dissolved in water describes that solution's _____.

3. A _____ is a way of separating substances in a solution that involves heating a liquid to a gas then collecting the solute that is left behind.

4. A _____ is a mixture whose substances are completely and evenly mixed, down to their individual molecules.

6. A _____ is a substance that dissolves in a solvent to make a solution.

7. A solution that has the greatest possible amount of substance dissolved in it is a _____ solution.

10. A solution that contains a large amount of solute is _____.

12. A _____ is a substance that can dissolve other substances.

14. A substance that can dissolve is said to be _____.

Student Guide

Motion

To understand how the world works, we must be able to describe and measure where things are and how they move. Then we can describe and measure how their locations change over time.

Lesson Objectives

- State the difference between *speed* and *velocity*.
- Describe how fast an object moves as the speed and direction of the object over time.
- Estimate speed by dividing the distance an object travels by the time it takes to travel that distance.
- Measure and graph the movement of an object's speed in a straight line.

PREPARE

Approximate lesson time is 60 minutes.

Materials

For the Student

> Average Speed for Each Interval
> Speed of a Moving Object
> marker - red
> meter stick
> newspaper - or magazines
> paper, 8 1/2" x 11" - graph
> pencil
> tape - masking - masking
> timer

Keywords and Pronunciations

frame of reference: An area from which a reference point is viewed.

motion: A change in an object's position. The motion of the car caused the passengers to lurch.

position: A point in space. The position of the minute hand on the clock changes every sixty seconds.

reference point: a point from which the position of other objects can be described

speed: How fast an object moves measured by how far it goes or would go in a chosen standard time interval. The go-cart raced to a speed of 20 kilometers per hour.

velocity (veh-LAH-suh-tee): An object's speed and direction. The velocity of the go-cart changed when the car rounded the curve.

159

LEARN

Activity 1: Measuring Location and Movement *(Online)*

Activity 2: Graphing the Speed of a Moving Object *(Online)*

Practice graphing speed by measuring distance and motion over a certain time period.

ASSESS

Lesson Assessment: Motion *(Offline)*

You will complete an offline assessment covering the main objectives of this lesson. Your learning coach will score this assessment.

LEARN

Activity 3: Optional: ZlugQuest Measurement *(Online)*

Name _____ Date _____

Motion

Average Speed for Each Interval

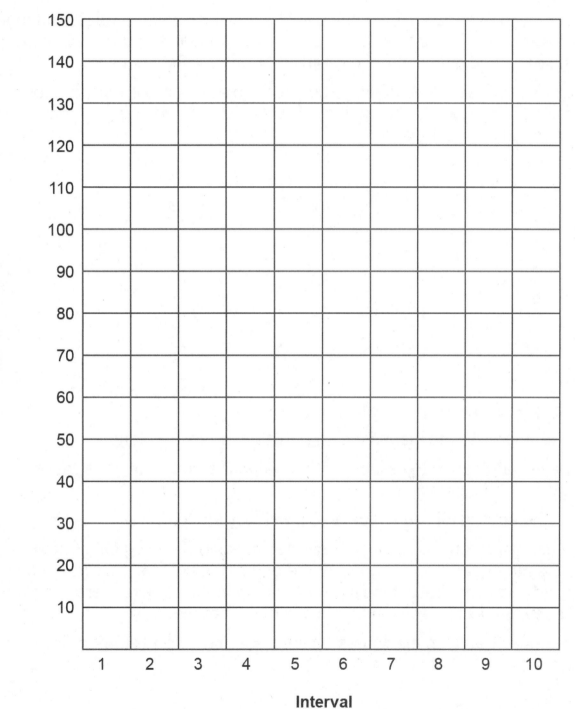

Name _____   Date _____

Motion

Speed of a Moving Object

The best way to understand something is to study it directly. By observing motion as it happens then graphing what you see, you can understand the relationship between speed and direction more clearly than by reading about it.

In this activity you will have a partner be your subject. You will study motion by creating a course on which the subject will walk. You will then graph your subject's speed on graph paper.

Materials:

Newspaper
Marker, red
Meter stick
Timer
Graph paper
Pencil
Masking tape

Procedure:

1. Find a large space or go outside.

2. Use the meter stick to measure a straight line, six meters long.

3. Lay newspaper along the six-meter line. Tape the pieces of newspaper together. This is your course.

4. If your meter stick folds up, tape it so it will stay straight.

Practice using the course. Have your subject walk slowly along the course tapping the meter stick to the paper. At the end of the course, have your subject turn around and come back, tapping the stick again. Make sure there is enough room for your subject to walk on both sides of the course.

Have the subject walk on the course again, speeding up and slowing down while walking.

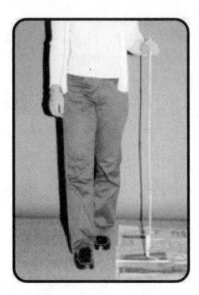

5. Tape the marker to the end of the meter stick with the cap removed.

6. Have your subject stand at the beginning of the course.

7. Tell your subject you will start the time and every two seconds, you will call out "NOW!" When you say "NOW!" the subject will tap the marker to the newspaper.

8. Instruct the subject to walk along the path and come back, changing speeds from fast to slow, still tapping the marker when you say "NOW!"

9. Start the timer. Stop after 20 seconds or when the subject reaches the end of the course.

Average Speed for the Whole Course

The subject should have made dots on the paper with the meter stick and marker.

Unfasten the marker and use the meter stick to measure the distance of each dot from the starting line. At the end of the course, where the subject stopped and turned, measure the turn by moving the meter stick as if you were measuring a square at the end of the path.

In the table, record each dot's distance from the starting line to get the total distance traveled. Cross out any leftover time your subject did not use.

Table 1

Time	Distance between red dots	Total distance from starting line
0 sec	0 cm	0 cm
2 sec		
4 sec		
6 sec		
8 sec		
10 sec		
12 sec		
14 sec		
16 sec		
18 sec		
20 sec		

Find the average speed of your subject by dividing the total distance traveled by the total time (20 seconds or however long it took to walk the course).

Subject's average speed: _____

Average Speed at Different Points on the Course

Now you'll need to calculate average speed at different points on the course. We'll call these points "intervals." The time between any two red dots is an interval. Every interval is two seconds long, no matter how close or far apart the dots are. The distance between 0 seconds and 2 seconds is interval 1. The distance between 2 seconds and 4 seconds is interval 2 and so on.

Write the distance between the red dots for each interval (you can copy these from Table 1). Then divide by two seconds (the time) to find the average speed for each interval. Round to the nearest centimeter. An example is done for you.

Table 2

Interval	Time	Distance between red dots	Seconds	Average speed in cm/sec
Example: 3	*5–7 sec*	*224 cm*	*÷ 2 seconds*	*112 cm/sec*
1	0–2 sec		÷ 2 seconds	
2	2–4 sec		÷ 2 seconds	
3	4–6 sec		÷ 2 seconds	
4	6–8 sec		÷ 2 seconds	
5	8–10 sec		÷ 2 seconds	
6	10–12 sec		÷ 2 seconds	
7	12–14 sec		÷ 2 seconds	
8	14–16 sec		÷ 2 seconds	
9	16–18 sec		÷ 2 seconds	
10	18–20 sec		÷ 2 seconds	

Analysis:

Use the graph titled "Average Speed for Each Interval" to graph the data in Table 2. For each interval, draw a bar to show the average speed for that interval.

Conclusion:

Use the graph to answer the questions below.

1. During which interval was the average speed fastest?

_____

2. During which interval was the average speed slowest?

_____

Student Guide
Mass and Force

Things remain as they are unless something pushes or pulls on them. These pushes and pulls are called *forces*. In this lesson you will investigate how some of the most common forces act in our world.

Lesson Objectives

- Describe the *mass* of an object as a measure of how hard it is to change its speed or direction.
- State that every push or pull (force) on one thing must make a balancing push or pull in the other direction on something else.
- State that objects keep moving with constant speed and direction unless there is an extra push or pull (force) to change their motion.
- Identify different "pushes" and "pulls" (electric, magnetic, muscular, spring-driven, wind-driven) as forces that can change an object's speed and direction.
- Identify the forces that are in balance when an object's speed and direction stay constant.

PREPARE

Approximate lesson time is 60 minutes.

Materials

For the Student

> Investigate Inertia
> household item - clothespin (spring type)
> pencil - very long and sharpened
> spoon
> toothpicks
> Thought Experiments: Forces

Keywords and Pronunciations

Galileo Galilei (gal-uh-LEE-oh gal-uh-LAY-ee)

inertia (ih-NUHR-shuh)

LEARN

Activity 1: Laws of Motion *(Online)*

Activity 2: Find the Forces *(Offline)*

Experiment with inertia and its relationship to forces by trying to prove the hypothesis in this investigation.

Safety

Your student may want to wear safety goggles while completing the Investigate Inertia activity.

Activity 3: Thought Experiments: Forces *(Offline)*

Thought experiments are designed so that the investigating takes place in your head. Investigate Newton's laws of motion by reading about some motion situations, then drawing conclusions.

ASSESS

Lesson Assessment: Mass and Force *(Offline)*

You will complete an offline assessment covering the main objectives of this lesson. Your learning coach will score this assessment.

LEARN

Activity 4: Optional: ZlugQuest Measurement *(Online)*

Name _____   Date _____

Mass and Force
Investigate Inertia

"Inertia" may sound like a strange word, but you actually have inertia all the time.

Imagine riding a subway train where passengers stand up during the trip. When the train moves forward, you lean backward. If the subway train suddenly slowed, you might be thrown forward. This happens because you yourself are in motion. When the train slows down, you tend to continue moving forward.

Inertia is the tendency for you to stay at rest if you, or any other object, are at rest. Inertia is also the tendency for you to stay in motion if you, or any other object, are in motion.

Now imagine you are riding the same subway train, your arms filled with packages or books. How would the starting and stopping motion of the train feel then? Because holding packages or books makes you more massive, you will feel the force of the movement of the subway less. You will not be thrown as far forward when the subway suddenly stops. Your inertia is greater, and the force of the subway stopping is not enough to overcome your inertia.

With the following experiment, try to prove this hypothesis:

The greater the inertia of an object, the less effect a force has on the object's motion.

Materials:

Clothespin (spring)
A very short, sharpened pencil
A long, sharpened pencil
Toothpick
Spoon

Procedure:

1. Be sure to do this activity on a flat, uncarpeted floor with an adult present. Make sure there is a lot of room around you.

2. Cut the toothpick so it fits into the clothespin as shown.

3. Lay the clothespin, pencils, and toothpick on the floor as shown.

4. Place your hand on the metal clasp to hold down the clothespin.

5. Use the edge of the spoon to knock out the toothpick.

6. Observe what happens.

7. Repeat the test two more times.

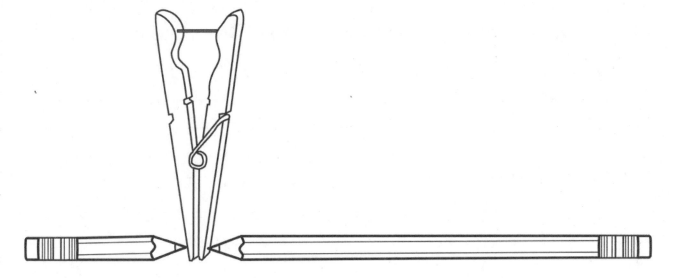

Observations and Analysis:

1. What did you observe?

_____

_____

2. Which object has greater inertia?

_____

_____

3. Is the force the same on each pencil? Explain.

_____

_____

_____

_____

_____

Conclusion:

1. The hypothesis for this investigation is:

   The greater the inertia of an object, the less effect a force has on the object's motion.

   Explain whether or not you proved this hypothesis. Give examples from your experiment.

   _____

   _____

   _____

   _____

   _____

Name _____   Date _____

Mass and Force
Thought Experiments: Forces

Before the start of an investigation, scientists spend some time sorting out their ideas and deciding on their hypotheses. They think about possible outcomes and develop a plan. They picture their experiments in their minds before beginning. These are called "thought experiments." By conducting thought experiments, you can train your brain to think about what could happen in investigations where you don't have the equipment or resources to actually conduct the experiment.

Experiment 1

A moving object will keep moving in a straight line without slowing or speeding up unless a force is applied to it. The force could speed it up, slow it down, or change its direction.

Diagram 1

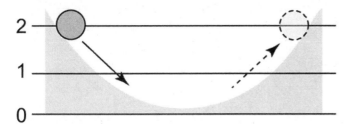

A ball rolling down the slope in Diagram 1 will roll up the slope to just about the same height—2 m.

Diagram 2

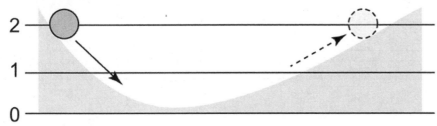

The ball in Diagram 2 does the same thing, but look how far it goes.

Diagram 3

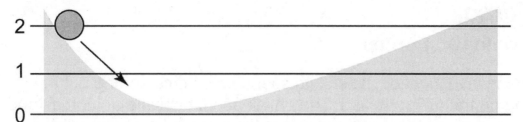

1. Look closely at Diagram 3. How far do you think the ball would go in this diagram? Draw your answer on the diagram.

Diagram 4

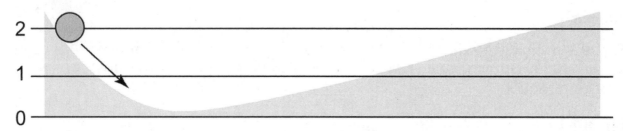

2. How far will the ball go in Diagram 4? Draw your answer on the diagram.

Diagram 5

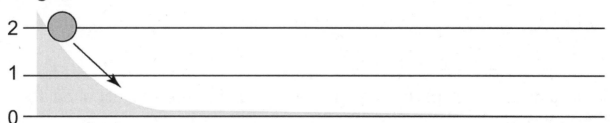

3. What about Diagram 5? Does the ball need any force to keep moving along the straight path?

_____

_____

Experiment 2

4. Roller skating is a hobby that can be done on many surfaces—on a street, a pavement, or in a roller skating rink on a wooden floor. If you begin roller skating, you will continue until a force stops you. What force could stop a rolling roller skater?

_____

_____

172

The diagrams below show what would happen to a roller skater on different surfaces. How far the roller skater rolls depends on the surface on which she is moving.

5. Study the diagrams and label each with the correct surface from the list: grass, concrete pavement, a wooden floor, a surface with no friction, and a living room carpet.

a. Surface _____

b. Surface _____

c. Surface _____

d. Surface _____

e. Surface _____

A. Surface _____

B. Surface _____

C. Surface _____

D. Surface _____

E. Surface _____

6. If there were no forces acting on the roller skater, what would happen to her motion?

_____

_____

Experiment 3

7. Now, turn your attention to the force of gravity. During the Apollo space missions, Alan B. Shepherd hit a golf ball on the Moon. The Moon is about 1/6 the size of the Earth. Its gravity is also 1/6 the force of gravity on Earth. A golf ball hit on the moon will fly higher and farther than on Earth. Why?

    _____

    _____

8. Imagine hitting a golf ball in the emptiness of space, where there is no gravity. What will happen to the ball?

    _____

    _____

Experiment 4

9. Diagram 1 displays someone holding a weight. Why doesn't the weight fall? Use the word "force" in your answer.

    1.

    _____

    _____

10. In Diagram 2, the added weight, weight B, takes the place of your hand. Weight A does not move. Why?

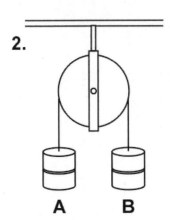

2.

A   B

_____

_____

11. In Diagram 3, what will happen to weight A? Why?

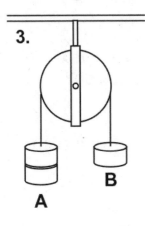

3.

A

B

_____

_____

12. In Diagram 4, what will happen to weight A? Why?

4.

_____

_____

Experiment 5

13. A boy is riding a bike on a straight road. He stops pedaling and lets the bike coast freely in a straight line. What force will cause the bike to stop?

_____

14. Imagine that the bike starts moving faster. How does the force of friction compare to the force of the boy pedaling?

_____

_____

Conclusions

Fill in the blanks to explain the conclusions you reached in these thought experiments.

15. A _____ is needed to start an object moving. An object with more mass will need _____ to start moving.

16. An object will continue to _____ in a _____ until another force acts on it.

17. An object will stay at rest if there are _____.

Student Guide

Potential and Kinetic Energy

If you place a ball on a table, even if the ball just sits there, it has a kind of energy. Why? Because if you give it a slight nudge, it can roll off the table, fall, and hit the floor. When it is on the table, it has energy because of its position. When it is falling, it is changing its energy of position to the energy of movement.

Lesson Objectives

- State that all the energy in a system added together always stays constant (is conserved).
- State that energy is the ability to do work.
- Explain the difference between potential energy and kinetic energy.
- In a moving system, identify where the kinetic and potential energies are contained.
- Recognize that a force acting over a distance changes the energy of an object.
- Ask questions or predict outcomes about the changes in energy that occur when objects collide.

PREPARE

Approximate time is 60 minutes.

Materials

For the Student

Kinetic or Potential?
Let's Roll!
book
marble
marker
ruler, standard
index cards - 3" x 5" (3)
paper towels - tube
scissors, round-end safety
tape - masking – masking
Colliding Coins
pennies (2)

Optional

Swing Low
metal washers (10)
paper clip
stopwatch
string
tape – masking

Keywords and Pronunciations

energy: The ability to do work; energy can take many forms, including movement, sound energy, heat energy, light energy, electricity, chemical energy, and nuclear energy

joule (jool)

kinetic energy (kuh-NEH-tihk): The energy of an object in motion. A moving swing's kinetic energy is greatest at the swing's lowest point, where its speed is greatest.

potential energy: The energy of an object due to its position. When you lift a rock off the ground, it now has potential energy.

LEARN

Activity 1: Energy Works! *(Online)*

Activity 2: Kinetic or Potential? *(Offline)*

Everywhere you look, energy is being transferred and work is being done. Think about the everyday things you do and sights you see. Decide whether potential or kinetic energy is at work.

Activity 3: Let's Roll! Kinetic and Potential Energy *(Offline)*

Explore the interactions between potential and kinetic energy with some classic energy experiments. Roll a marble down a ramp. Then, change the angle of the ramp to see how potential energy changes.

Activity 4: Colliding Coins *(Online)*

Read Energy in Action to prepare for this activity. You will then complete the Colliding Coins assignment. This assignment requires you to predict the potential and kinetic energy transfer between pennies that collide.

ASSESS

Lesson Assessment: Potential and Kinetic Energy *(Offline)*

You will complete an offline assessment covering the main objectives of this lesson. Your learning coach will score this assessment.

LEARN

Activity 5: Optional: Swing Low *(Offline)*

This activity is OPTIONAL. It's provided for enrichment or extra practice, but not required for completion of this lesson. You may skip this activity.

Swinging a pendulum is another easy way to study potential and kinetic energy. See what happens as you make changes to the length of a pendulum swing.

Name _____   Date _____

Potential and Kinetic Energy
Kinetic or Potential?

Read the descriptions of energy below. Label each as either kinetic (KE) or potential (PE).

_____ a strong wind

_____ the moving gases of a burning candle

_____ a pushed-down spring

_____ a rock at the top of a hill

_____ a pulled bow ready to shoot an arrow

_____ the moving parts of an ocean wave

_____ sound waves from a beeping horn

_____ a battery

_____ a thrown basketball

_____ the moving strong winds of a tornado

_____ a stretched rubber band

_____ an unlit match

_____ an apple hanging on a tree limb

_____ a spinning pinwheel

Name _____   Date _____

Potential and Kinetic Energy
Let's Roll

At the end of a race, the winning runner must run through tape stretched across the finish line. In order to break the tape in half, the runner must transfer enough energy from himself to the tape to tear it. Walking to the tape and saying, "Okay, I'm finished now," won't be enough to break it. Increasing his speed by running across the finish line increases the runner's energy. The energy of a moving object depends partly on its speed.

Which will move a target farther, a fast marble or a slow one?

Hypothesis:

Write your hypothesis below. Avoid using the words "I think." (Your hypothesis already says what you think.)

_____

_____

_____

_____

Materials:

Paper towel tube

Scissors

Ruler

Marker

Books or soda can

Masking tape

3 x 5 index cards, 3

Marble

Masking tape

Procedure:

1. Cut the paper towel tube in half lengthwise.

2. Make a mark on the inside of the tube for every centimeter. Label them "1," 2," and so on.

3. On a flat surface, use the books to prop up the tube so the top is about 10 – 12 centimeters above the table. The highest centimeter mark should be at the top of the tube.

4. Make sure the bottom of the tube touches the table. Use tape to secure the tube.

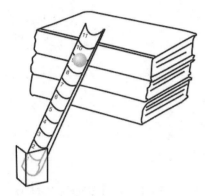

5. Place the index cards on top of one another. Fold them in half lengthwise, resembling a book.

6. Place the cards at the end of the tube, touching the tube with the inside fold facing the top. This is your target.

7. Place the marble at the top of the tube and let it roll down. Make sure your marble does not escape under the bottom of the cards.

8. Measure the distance the crease of the note card moved from the end of the tube. Record your data in the table

9. Repeat steps 5 to 8 for every 5 centimeters on the tube.

Scientist Notebook:

Variables:

Write the independent variable (what is changed by the experimenter):

_____

_____

Write the dependent variable (what happens because of the change):

_____

_____

The first height from which you release the marble will be your control. You will compare all your other tests to the distance the target moved after you released the marble from the highest centimeter mark.

Starting point on the tube in centimeters	Distance target moved in centimeters

Analysis

Make a line graph to show the relationship between where you placed the marble and how far the target moved each time you let it roll down the tube. You will need to add numbers to the graph based on your data.

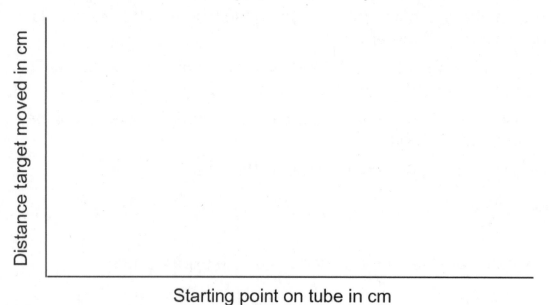

1. What is the relationship between where you released the marble and how far the target moved?

_____

_____

2. At which location did the marble have more speed when released, at the top of the tube or the bottom?

_____

_____

3. At which location did the marble have the most potential energy? The least?

_____

_____

4. At which point did potential energy convert to kinetic energy?

_____

_____

5. At which location did the marble have the least kinetic energy? The most?

_____

_____

Conclusion

Use evidence from your investigation to explain how speed affects the energy of a moving object.

_____

_____

_____

_____

_____

_____

_____

_____

Name _____   Date _____

Assignment

Colliding Coins

When two objects collide, energy is transferred from one object to another. In this investigation, you will explore how kinetic energy can be transferred from one coin to another.

Materials:

- 2 pennies
- a smooth, flat surface

Procedure:

1. Be sure to do this activity on a flat, smooth surface, such as a floor or table. Make sure there is a lot of room around you.

2. Place the two pennies on the table. What type of energy do they possess?

   _____

3. Brainstorm: What are some ways you can transfer energy between the two pennies? Record your ideas here.

   _____

   _____

4. How will you know that energy has been transferred?

   _____

   _____

5. Test your ideas. Were you able to make the second penny move? _____

6. Using your finger, flick one penny so it slides and bumps into the second penny. What did you observe?

   _____

   _____

7. Predict. How will lowering the kinetic energy of Penny 1 affect the energy transferred to Penny 2?

_____

_____

8. Repeat Step 6 two more times, changing the speed of the first penny. How does changing the kinetic energy of Penny 1 affect Penny 2?

_____

_____

Analysis:

1. What type of energy does Penny 1 have while it is in motion? What type of energy does it have after it collides with Penny 2?

_____

_____

2. Energy is always conserved. Where did the kinetic energy from Penny 1 go? Explain.

_____

_____

3. Would a car moving at 50 mph have more or less kinetic energy than a car moving at 25 mph? Explain.

_____

_____

_____

_____

Name _____   Date _____

Potential and Kinetic Energy
Swing Low

What factors are important in the speed of a pendulum swing? Try changing a pendulum's length and mass to see which results in a faster swing.

Hypothesis:

Write what you think will happen if you change a pendulum's mass (without saying "I think").

_____

_____

Write what you think will happen if you change the length of the pendulum's string (without saying "I think").

_____

_____

Materials:

Paper clip   Stopwatch
10 metal washers   Tape
String   Ruler

Procedure:

1. Tie the paper clip to one end of the string. Tape the other end to the corner of a table so the paper clip swings freely when it is pulled back.

2. Open the paper clip so washers can be slid onto it. Place one washer on the paper clip.

3. Pull the washer back a few centimeters and let go. Time 5 complete swings (from the starting point to when it swings all the way back to the starting point). Record your observations in the chart.

4. Place 5 washers on the paper clip and time 5 complete swings of 10 washers.

5. Repeat step 3 with 10 washers.

6. Now, shorten the pendulum string in half. Time 5 complete swings of 10 washers. Record your data.

7. Shorten the pendulum string in half again. Time 5 complete swings. Record your data.

Observations:

Table 1

Number of Washers	Time for 5 Swings	Time for 1 Swing (Divide time for 5 swings by 5.)

Table 2

Length of Pendulum String	Time for 5 Swings of 10 Washers	Time for 1 Swing (Divide time for 5 swings by 5.)

Analysis:

Which seemed to have more effect on the pendulum swing: adding weight or changing the length of the string?

_____

_____

Conclusion:

Re-read both hypotheses. Do your tests support your hypotheses? Explain whether or not you proved both hypotheses.

_____

_____

_____

187

Student Guide

Simple Machines and Work

Lifting a stone out of the ground can be a hard task. But you can make it easier with a lever. You can lift the stone without as much effort then because you have used a simple machine. In doing so, you have shown that the work equation really does. . .well. . .work!

Lesson Objectives

- Describe how simple machines change the work-distance relationship to make effort easier.
- Describe examples of simple machines in everyday life.

PREPARE

Approximate lesson time is 60 minutes.

Materials

For the Student

> Forces and Levers
> marker
> ruler, standard
> coins - same currency (10)
> tape - masking
> It's an Inclined Plane
> book - large (5)
> food - 240 mL of rice
> household item - twist tie
> rubber band
> measuring cup
> ruler, metric
> scissors, round-end safety

Keywords and Pronunciations

effort force: The force that pushes on one arm of the lever. The effort force of a shovel is less than the resultant force of lifting dirt.

fulcrum (FUHL-kruhm)**:** The pivot of a lever. Alice used the ground as a fulcrum when she lifted the dirt with a shovel.

lever: A simple machine that has five components: fulcrum, effort force, resistance force, load, and bar. A seesaw is a kind of lever.

load: The weight that is lifted by the lever. A scoop of dirt is the load lifted by a shovel.

resistant force: The force exerted by a lever on an object. The resistance force can be less than the effort force when you use a simple machine.

LEARN

Activity 1: Force and Work in Action *(Online)*

Activity 2: Investigating Forces with Levers *(Offline)*

Multiply forces using coins and a simple lever. Learning about the forces involved in levers can be tricky, but a demonstration will make it easier to understand.

Activity 3: It's an Inclined Plane *(Offline)*

Investigate one type of simple machine: the inclined plane. Inclined planes also decrease the force needed to move an object. Observe this effect of an inclined plane.

ASSESS

Lesson Assessment: Simple Machines and Work *(Offline)*

You will complete an offline assessment covering the main objectives of this lesson. Your learning coach will score this assessment.

Name _____   Date _____

Simple Machines and Work
Forces and Levers

A balance is a special kind of lever. You can use a balance to demonstrate how levers change the amount of force needed to lift an object. You can also see that using a lever increases the distance over which that force is used.

Materials:

Ruler

Marker

Tape

Coins (5 to 10, same currency)

Procedure

1. Balance the ruler across the marker. You may need to secure the marker to the table with tape. Where is the fulcrum?

2. Place a coin on either side, close to the fulcrum to balance the lever.

3. Stack one coin on a side. Notice that side moves downward.

4. Try to lift the heavier load by moving the single coin on the opposite side.

5. Continue adding weight to the same side, one coin at a time. Continue moving the coin on the opposite side of the balance.

You should be able to lift the heavier loads by moving the single coin farther and farther away from the fulcrum. This is how a lever works: it can lift heavier and heavier loads but it must do so over a longer distance. As you move the coin farther away from the fulcrum, you increase the distance over which the force is applied.

Investigation Idea

Experiment with moving the fulcrum to either end of the lever. Try using coins of different sizes and masses.

Review

1. Label the effort force, resistance force, load, and fulcrum on this lever.

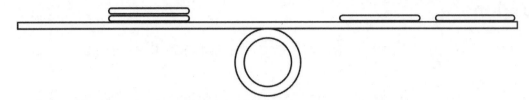

2. Oversized packages may be delivered in large wooden crates. The top of the crates must be pried open. Would you use a short crowbar or long crowbar to pry open the crate? Why?

_____

_____

_____

_____

Name _____ Date _____

Simple Machines and Work
It's an Inclined Plane

Another simple machine is an inclined plane. It is a flat surface that is higher at one end.

Ramps are examples of inclined planes. You can use a ramp to lift objects to a higher place. Less force is needed to move objects using an inclined plane.

Materials:

Large books
Ruler
240 mL of rice in a small plastic bag
Twist tie
Rubber band
Scissors

Procedure:

1. Close the plastic bag with the twist tie.

2. Cut the rubber band to make a rubber band strip. Tie the rubber band strip to the top of the bag.

3. Stack the books in a pile.

4. Create an inclined plane by leaning one book against the pile.

5. Set the bag of rice on the table.

6. Hold the end of the rubber band and lift the rice straight up to the top of the book stack. Do not use the inclined plane.

7. Use the ruler to measure the length of the rubber band. Record your data in centimeters in the table.

8. Place the bag at the bottom of the inclined plane.

9. Pull on the rubber band to drag the bag to the top of the stack.

10. When it is almost at the top, measure the length of the rubber band.

11. Repeat steps 6 to 10 one time. Record your data in the table.

Observations	Trial 1	Trial 2
Length of rubber band lifting		
Length of rubber band using inclined plane		

Conclusion

1. What simple machine was used in this experiment?

_____

_____

2. Why was the rubber band stretched longer when you lifted the bag straight up in the air?

_____

_____

3. Did using the inclined plane take less force or more force to move the bag?

_____

_____

Student Guide

Engineering and Design, Part 1

How good are you at solving problems? How good are you at designing a solution to solve a problem? There is a process to follow that helps guide you through solving a problem. You will be given a problem to solve using your understanding of magnets. Let's get started!

Lesson Objectives

- Define a simple design problem reflecting a need or a want that includes specified criteria for success and constraints on materials, time, or cost.
- Generate or compare multiple possible solutions to a problem based on how well each is likely to meet the criteria and constraints of the problem.
- Plan and carry out fair tests in which variables are controlled and failure points are considered to identify aspects of a model or prototype that can be improved.

PREPARE

Approximate time is 60 minutes.

Materials

For the Student

Engineering Design Graded Assignment

Keywords and Pronunciations

constraint: A limitation to a design

LEARN

LEARN

Activity 1: Engineering Design *(Online)*

Instructions

Navigate through the steps in the design process. Follow the examples given in the activity to help illustrate the design process.

Activity 2: Using the Design Process *(Online)*

Instructions

Come up with a design that will enable you to raise a book off of the floor with just one finger. Work in the Engineering Design Assignment and complete the first 3 steps. Please submit your work for this assignment to the teacher if requested.

Activity 3: Lesson Review *(Online)*

Name _____   Date _____

Graded Assignment

Engineering Design

Total Score: _____ of 20 points

This assignment will require you to use the design process to solve a problem using simple machines.

Problem: Using only household materials, design a simple machine that can lift a book off the floor with just one finger.

(Score for Question 1: ___ of 2 points)

1. **Identify the problem**. Write the problem statement.

    _____

    _____

    _____

    _____

(Score for Question 2: ___ of 2 points)

2. **Define criteria for the solution**. This means that you figure out the different parts of a solution that fix the problem. Whatever the solution is, it needs to meet certain goals.

    _____

    _____

    _____

    _____

(Score for Question 3: ___ of 2 points)

3. **Describe some constraints for the design**. Constraints are limitations to a design. Time and money are typical constraints. This step is to try and figure out and work around problems and be prepared. It would be great to have unlimited resources, but that rarely happens in real life. As a student, one of your constraints would be that you are only using household items.

    _____

    _____

    _____

    _____

(Score for Question 4: ___ of 2 points)

4. **Do background research on simple machines.** Suggest two simple machines you could use for your solution.

_____

_____

_____

_____

(Score for Question 5: ___ of 2 points)

5. **Brainstorm and write down two or three solutions.**

_____

_____

_____

_____

(Score for Question 6: ___ of 2 points)

6. **Analyze the possible solutions. List the solution that will work best.**

_____

_____

(Score for Question 7: ___ of 2 points)

7. **Build and test one of the solutions (on a small scale).** Draw a sketch of your design. If you need more space, use a separate sheet of paper.

(Score for Question 8: ___ of 2 points)

8. Write your observations from the test.

_____

_____

_____

_____

(Score for Question 9: ___ of 2 points)

9. Analyze the results of the test. Was your device successful? What did you learn from the test? What problems or failure points came up?

_____

_____

_____

_____

_____

(Score for Question 10: ___ of 2 points)

10. Suggest improvements based on the analysis. Write down suggestions to improve the device based on your analysis.

_____

_____

_____

_____

_____

Student Guide
Engineering and Design, Part 2

Many times people recognize that there is a problem and talk about it, but they fail to come up with a solution. During the last lesson, you came up with a problem, constraints of the problem, and criteria for a solution. The time has come to dig in and solve the problem.

Lesson Objectives

- Define a simple design problem reflecting a need or a want that includes specified criteria for success and constraints on materials, time, or cost.
- Generate or compare multiple possible solutions to a problem based on how well each is likely to meet the criteria and constraints of the problem.
- Plan and carry out fair tests in which variables are controlled and failure points are considered to identify aspects of a model or prototype that can be improved.

PREPARE

Approximate time is 60 minutes.

Materials

For the Student

    Engineering Design Graded Assignment

Keywords and Pronunciations

constraint: A limitation to a design

LEARN

Activity 1: Engineering Design *(Online)*

Navigate through the steps in the design process. Follow the examples given in the activity to help illustrate the design process.

Activity 2: Test, Evaluate and Improve *(Online)*

Come up with a design that will enable you to raise a book off of the floor with just one finger. Work in the Engineering Design Assignment and complete the final steps. Please submit your work for this assignment to the teacher if requested.

Activity 3: Lesson Review *(Online)*

Name _____   Date _____

Graded Assignment

Engineering Design

Total Score: _____ of 20 points

This assignment will require you to use the design process to solve a problem using simple machines.

Problem: Using only household materials, design a simple machine that can lift a book off the floor with just one finger.

(Score for Question 1: ___ of 2 points)

1. **Identify the problem**. Write the problem statement.

_____

_____

_____

_____

(Score for Question 2: ___ of 2 points)

2. **Define criteria for the solution**. This means that you figure out the different parts of a solution that fix the problem. Whatever the solution is, it needs to meet certain goals.

_____

_____

_____

_____

(Score for Question 3: ___ of 2 points)

3. **Describe some constraints for the design**. Constraints are limitations to a design. Time and money are typical constraints. This step is to try and figure out and work around problems and be prepared. It would be great to have unlimited resources, but that rarely happens in real life. As a student, one of your constraints would be that you are only using household items.

_____

_____

_____

_____

(Score for Question 4: ___ of 2 points)

4. **Do background research on simple machines.** Suggest two simple machines you could use for your solution.

_____

_____

_____

_____

(Score for Question 5: ___ of 2 points)

5. **Brainstorm and write down two or three solutions.**

_____

_____

_____

_____

(Score for Question 6: ___ of 2 points)

6. **Analyze the possible solutions. List the solution that will work best.**

_____

_____

(Score for Question 7: ___ of 2 points)

7. **Build and test one of the solutions (on a small scale).** Draw a sketch of your design. If you need more space, use a separate sheet of paper.

(Score for Question 8: ___ of 2 points)

8.   **Write your observations from the test**.

_____

_____

_____

_____

(Score for Question 9: ___ of 2 points)

9.   **Analyze the results of the test**. Was your device successful? What did you learn from the test? What problems or failure points came up?

_____

_____

_____

_____

_____

(Score for Question 10: ___ of 2 points)

10.   **Suggest improvements based on the analysis.** Write down suggestions to improve the device based on your analysis.

_____

_____

_____

_____

_____

Student Guide

Optional: Motion in a Circle

This lesson is OPTIONAL. It's provided for enrichment or extra practice, but not required for completion of this unit. You may skip this lesson.

Lesson Objectives

- Explain the forces at work that will cause an object to move in a circle.
- Predict how the motion of an object will change if the force applied to the object is more or less, or the speed of the object is faster or slower, or both.
- State that if the force holding an object in a circular motion suddenly falls to zero, the object will continue to move in a straight line with the same energy.

PREPARE

Approximate lesson time is 60 minutes.

Materials

For the Student

> Setting It Straight
> marble
> paper - strip (3 cm by 20 cm)
> pencil
> plate, paper - smooth with raised lip
> scissors, round-end safety
> tape - masking
> The Spin Is In
> washers (3)
> spring scale
> string - 30 cm

Keywords and Pronunciations

acceleration: Any change in velocity. An airplane taking off and a person riding a carousel horse moving at constant speed are both experiencing acceleration.

centrifugal (sen-TRIH-fyuh-guhl)

centrifuge (SEN-trih-fyooj)

centripetal force (sen-TRIH-puh-tl)**:** A force directed at the center of a circle, which pulls or pushes objects toward the center. When you swing a ball on a string in a circle, a centripetal force is acting on the ball.

inertia (ih-NUHR-shuh)

tangential (tan-JENT-shuhl)

velocity (veh-LAH-suh-tee)**:** A description of an object's speed and direction. Either a change in speed or a change in direction will cause in a change in velocity.

LEARN

Activity 1: Optional: Round and Round We Go *(Online)*

When an object moves in a circle, the forces involved are a bit more complicated than those that keep an object moving in a straight line. If you don't think so, imagine yourself in a roller-coaster car going around a curve. You slide to the side of the car. What is going on? Perform simple tests to find out.

Activity 2: Optional: Setting It Straight *(Offline)*

Does an object moving in a circle really tend to move in a straight line when there's no longer any centripetal force? This is hard to believe. The best way to find out is to test it. Use a marble, paper plate, and a target to set this idea straight in your mind.

Activity 3: Optional: The "Spin" Is In on Centripetal Force *(Offline)*

Does all this talk of forces have your head spinning? Investigate the force involved in spinning an object in a circle. You'll understand the forces behind looping roller coasters, space satellites, and our spinning Earth.

Safety

Perform this activity in a wide, open space. Keep other people away from your student as she performs this activity.

Name _____   Date _____

Motion in a Circle
Setting It Straight

When objects move in a circle, a force is at work. This force is called *centripetal force*. Centripetal force keeps objects moving in a circle by continually pulling the object towards the center of the circle.

Materials

Strip of paper (3 cm by 20 cm)

Pencil

Tape

Paper plate – smooth surface and raised lip around the edge

Scissors

Marble

Procedure

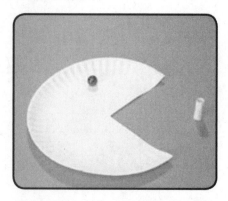

1. Wrap the strip of paper around the pencil. Tape the cylinder made by the paper. This is the target.

2. Cut a pie-shaped wedge from the paper plate. The wedge should be about ¼ of the plate.

3. Secure the plate to a table with tape.

4. Place the target on the table about 15 cm away from the open edge of the plate. Try to put the target in a place where you think the marble will hit it after rolling around the plate and then rolling off the opening.

5. Roll the marble smoothly along the inside of the plate. Observe what happens to the target.

6. Try moving the target or rolling the marble the other way around the plate.

Questions:

1. The marble rolls in a circle around the plate. What force pushes the marble to the center? _____

2. Explain the role of centripetal force as the marble rolled around the plate.

   _____

   _____

3. Describe what happened when the marble rolled off the plate.

   _____

   _____

Name _____   Date _____

Motion in a Circle
The Spin Is In

You've learned about the effects of centripetal force. Now investigate the results of applying varying amounts of this force.

Materials

Washers – 3

Spring scale

Procedure

1. Tie the washers to the end of the string.

2. With one hand, swing the washers around in a circle in front of your body.

3. Try swinging the washers faster and slower. Notice the amount of force you need to use to swing the washers at different speeds.

4. Tie the other end of the string to the spring scale.

5. Hold the top of the spring scale and swing the washers as before.

6. Swing the washers faster and slower.

Questions:

1. What did you notice about the amount of force needed to swing the washers at different speeds? Was it a pushing force or a pulling force?

_____

_____

2. How did the spring scale behave when you swung the washers at different speeds?

_____

_____

3. What does the behavior of the spring scale tell you about the amount of force needed to move any object in a circle at fast and slow speeds?

_____

_____

To Think About

When you swing the washers, you should feel the pull of the string. That's the object pulling on you. The string pulls on the object, keeping it moving in a circle.

Student Guide

Optional: Gravity and Motion Between Planets and Beyond!

This lesson is OPTIONAL. It's provided for enrichment or extra practice, but not required for completion of this unit. You may skip this lesson.

Lesson Objectives

- Describe the role of gravity in maintaining a planet's orbit around the sun.
- Define weight as the result of the force of gravity on mass.

PREPARE

Approximate lesson time is 60 minutes.

Materials

For the Student

  Gravity in Space

Keywords and Pronunciations

acceleration: Any change in velocity. An airplane taking off and a person riding a carousel horse moving at constant speed are both experiencing acceleration.

elliptical (ih-LIP-tih-kuhl)

gravity: The force that pulls objects down to the Earth. When you jump into the air, the force of gravity pulls you back down.

mass: The amount of matter in an object, or a measure of how hard it is to change an object´s speed or direction. The mass of the ball was 50 grams, and Earth´s gravity acted on this mass.

weight: The result of the force of gravity on mass. The astronauts weighed six times more on Earth than they did on the moon.

LEARN

Activity 1: Optional: Gravity in Our Universe *(Online)*

Gravitation pulls you toward the center of the Earth and pulls the Earth toward the sun. But gravitation exists between any two objects, not just very large ones. There's a gravitational force between you and your bed, between two pencils, even between two atoms. How does gravitation operate in our universe? How is it responsible for Earth's orbit around the sun? How does gravitation change on other planets? Calculate the weight of objects on Earth and in the solar system.

Activity 2: Optional: Gravity in Space *(Online)*

If you are interested in a miracle diet, plan a trip to Mercury where you'll weigh one-third less! Want to bulk up? Visit Jupiter and increase your weight almost three times! The weight of objects on different planets changes due to the forces of gravity existing on each planet.

Name _____   Date _____

Gravity and Motion Between Planets and Beyond!
Gravity in Space

Answer the questions after visiting the Exploratorium online. Use the information at the site to help you.

1. Give your weight on the planetary bodies listed below:

    (a) Mercury _____

    (b) Venus _____

    (c) Moon _____

    (d) Mars _____

    (e) Jupiter _____

    (f) Saturn _____

    (g) Uranus _____

    (h) Neptune _____

2. Consider only the eight planets and the moon. On which planet did you weigh the most? The least? What does this tell you about their gravitational force and masses?

    _____

    _____

3. If you were floating in space, what would be your weight? Would you have mass? Explain.

    _____

    _____

CHALLENGE

4. Jupiter is 318 times more massive than Earth, but your weight on Jupiter was not exactly 318 times your weight on Earth. Why is this?

    _____

    _____

Student Guide

Motion and Forces: Unit Review and Assessment

Participate in a different kind of scavenger hunt to review what you've learned about motion and forces. Review new words with a crossword puzzle, and if you wish, make a motion machine. Then, take the Unit Assessment. It promises to be a very "moving" experience.

Lesson Objectives

- Demonstrate mastery of the objectives taught in this unit.
- Describe how simple machines change the work-distance relationship to make effort easier.
- Describe the *mass* of an object as a measure of how hard it is to change its speed or direction.
- State that every push or pull (force) on one thing must make a balancing push or pull in the other direction on something else.
- State the difference between speed and *velocity*.
- Describe examples of simple machines in everyday life.
- Explain the difference between *potential energy* and *kinetic energy*.

PREPARE

Approximate lesson time is 60 minutes.

Advance Preparation

- A styrofoam meat tray is needed for this activity. You can find them at any grocery store. Some stores will give you many trays at no cost if you explain that they are needed for a science lesson.

Materials

For the Student

Motion and Forces Crossword

Optional

Motion Machine Madness
household item - balloon
household item - flexible straw
household item - marker
household item - pins (4)
household item - rubber band
household item - styrofoam meat tray
compass - drawing
ruler, metric
scissors, round-end safety
tape - masking
Question Review Table

LEARN

Activity 1: Unit Review (Online)

Activity 2: Motion and Forces Crossword (Offline)

Complete a crossword puzzle to review some of those "heavy" facts you learned in this unit!

Activity 3: Optional: Motion Machine Madness (Offline)

This activity is OPTIONAL. It's provided for enrichment or extra practice, but not required for completion of this lesson. You may skip this activity.

Try a new way to review—make a motion machine! Make an air-powered vehicle that will help you explain some of the things you've learned in this unit about motion and forces. You may find a "hands-on" approach a good way to review.

ASSESS

Unit Assessment: Motion and Forces (Offline)

Complete an offline Unit Assessment. Your learning coach will score the assessment.

LEARN

Activity 4: Unit Assessment Review Table (Online)

If you earned a score of less than 80% on the Unit Assessment, complete the activity.

If you earned a score of 80% or greater, you may skip this activity.

Let's prepare to retake the Unit Assessment:

- Print the Question Review Table.

- Identify the questions that you answered incorrectly.

- Complete the appropriate review activities listed in the table.

Note: This will guide you through the process of using the Unit Assessment Review Tables. You may skip this video if you've already viewed it in another unit or course. As always, check in with your student's teacher if you have any questions.

Activity 5: Optional: ZlugQuest Measurement (Online)

Name _____   Date _____

Motion and Forces: Unit Review and Assessment
Motion and Forces Crossword

Word Bank

mass	energy
speed	velocity
fulcrum	acceleration
lever	motion
resistant force	potential energy
effort force	kinetic energy
load	

Across

5. The amount of matter in an object, or a measure of how hard it is to get an object going.

6. A change in an object's position.

9. The force that pushes on one arm of a lever.

10. A simple machine made with a bar and fulcrum that makes work easier by spreading force out over a longer distance.

12. The force exerted by a lever on an object.

13. The ability to work.

Down

1. Any change in velocity, be it speed, direction, or both.

2. An object's speed and direction.

3. The energy of an object due to its position.

4. The energy of an object in motion.

7. A measure of how far an object goes, or would go, in a certain amount of time.

8. The weight that is lifted by a lever.

11. The pivot of a lever.

Name _____   Date _____

Motion and Forces: Unit Review and Assessment
Question Review Table

Before you retake the Unit Assessment, use the table to figure out which activities you should review.

Circle the numbers of the questions that you missed on the Unit Assessment. Review the activities that correspond with these questions.

Question	Lesson	Review Activity
1	2: Mass and Force	Laws of Motion Thought Experiments: Forces
2	1: Motion	Measuring Location and Movements
3	3: Potential and Kinetic Energy	Energy Works!
4	4: Simple Machines and Work	Force and Work in Action Investigation Forces with Levers It's an Inclined Plane
5, 6, 7	2: Mass and Force	Laws of Motion Thought Experiment: Forces Find the Forces
8, 9	3: Potential and Kinetic Energy	Energy Works! Kinetic or Potential? Let's Roll! Kinetic and Potential Energy
10	2: Mass and Force	Laws of Motion

Name _____ Date _____

Motion and Forces: Unit Review and Assessment
Motion Machine Madness

You can review many principles related to forces and motion by building your own motion machine. Follow the instructions to make the machine, then complete the activities for a fun review.

Materials:

pins, 4

foam meat tray

tape

flexible straw

scissors

drawing compass

marker

balloon

ruler

rubber band

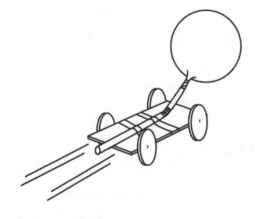

Procedure:

1. From the meat tray, cut a rectangle about 7.5 cm by 18 cm, keeping the edges as straight and parallel as possible.

2. Cut four circles, each 7.5 cm in diameter. Set the drawing compass at about 3.25 centimeters to make the circles.

3. Inflate the balloon a few times to stretch it. Place the nozzle over the straw nearest the flexible part.

4. Seal the nozzle securely with tape so you can inflate the balloon by blowing through the straw.

5. Tape the straw to the car as shown in the drawing.

6. Push one pin into the center of each circle and then into the edge of the rectangle. The pins are axles. It is okay if the wheels wobble. Do not push them in snugly as the wheels need to rotate freely.

7. Inflate the balloon and pinch the straw to hold in the air. Place the motion machine on a smooth surface and release the straw.

Review Exercises:

1. What is required to get the motion machine in motion?

_____

_____

2. When you first release the machine, how is potential energy converted to kinetic energy?

_____

_____

3. Every push or pull on one thing (action) results in a push or pull in the other direction on something else (reaction). What is the action and reaction that moves the machine forward?

_____

_____

4. At what point can you tell when the force of air ceases?

_____

_____

Student Guide

Forms of Energy

Think about all the types of energy that you use in your everyday life. You use energy, for instance, to heat your house, to light up your room, to move your car, to play sports and be active, and much more. Learn about many different forms of energy, how it's used, and how it changes.

Have you ever heard someone say they have no energy, or been told you have too much energy? Energy is all around us. We can't see all forms of it, but we can see it make things happen. Explore where most energy comes from, and what some of the different types of energy are.

Lesson Objectives

- Identify different forms of energy, such as light energy, heat energy, and mechanical energy.
- Recognize that energy is neither created nor destroyed.
- Recognize that energy is the ability to cause change in structure or motion.
- Identify the Earth's major source of energy as the sun.
- Recognize that energy can be stored for later use in many forms, such as in food, fuel, batteries, and stretched rubber bands.
- Recognize that energy from the sun makes life on Earth possible.
- Develop a model of waves to describe patterns in terms of amplitude and wavelength and that waves can cause objects to move.

PREPARE

Approximate time is 60 minutes.

Advance Preparation

This activity requires a metal washer. If you do not have one, you will need to purchase this item ahead of time.

Materials

For the Student

Energy in Action
rubber band
plastic wrap
masking tape
Slinky®
voice recording device
Light and Sound Waves Assignment

Keywords and Pronunciations

amplitude: How high a wave will rise or fall

energy: The ability to cause change in structure or motion. The energy in gasoline can be used to make a car mov

wave: A disturbance that travels from one location to another

wavelength: The distance between two like points on a wave

LEARN

Activity 1: Where Is Your Energy? *(Online)*

Activity 2: Identify and Explore Forms of Energy *(Offline)*

Overview

Energy is found in many places. Sometimes you can see it, as in the light energy of the lightning bolt that flashes across the sky. But can you see the energy stored in a battery? Energy can be stored in many ways other than in batteries. Explore some ways it can be stored and released in three "energizing" activities.

Activity Steps

Activity 1: Pendulum

1. Tie one end of a 20 cm piece of string to a rock or weight. Tie the other end of the string around a ruler.

2. Place the ruler on a table so that the end of the ruler with the string tied to it hangs over the edge of the table. Place a few books on the other end of the ruler to hold it in place. The string with the weight should hang straight down to the floor.

3. Make the pendulum swing by pulling the rock to one side and letting it go again.

Activity 2: Spool Toy

1. Thread a rubber band through the inside of a spool. On one end, put the short toothpick through the loop of the rubber band to hold it in place.

2. Turn the spool over. Place a washer on the spool so that the rubber band can be pulled through the center. Place the long toothpick through the loop of the rubber band.

3. Place the toy on a flat surface so that the short toothpick is on the bottom. Using the long toothpick, turn the rubber band five times. When you let go, watch what happens to the spool toy.

4. Repeat Step 3 a few more times. Change the number of times you turn the rubber band with each test.

<u>Activity 3: Chemical Changes</u>

1. Take a piece of steel wool about the size of a quarter and place it around the bulb of a thermometer so the steel wool touches the bulb. After five minutes, record the temperature shown on the thermometer.

2. This is the starting temperature of the steel wool.

3. Place the steel wool in the cup and pour enough vinegar over it to cover it.

4. After five minutes, squeeze the excess vinegar out of the steel wool and place it again around the bulb of the thermometer.

5. Watch the temperature for a few minutes and record the highest temperature reading.

Activity 3: Light and Sound Energy *(Online)*

Instructions

Read Big Universe Sound Waves and Communication. Open and complete the Light and Sound Waves Investigation activity.

ASSESS

Lesson Assessment: Forms of Energy *(Online)*

You will complete an online assessment covering the main objectives of this lesson.

Name _____   Date _____

Forms of Energy
Energy in Action

Overview

Energy is found in many places. Sometimes you can see it, as in the light energy of the lightning bolt that flashes across the sky. But can you see the energy stored in a battery? Energy can be stored in many ways other than in batteries. Explore some of these ways it can be stored and released in three "energizing" activities.

Activity 1: Pendulum

1. Tie one end of a 20 cm long piece of string to a rock or weight. Tie the other end of the string around a ruler.

2. Place the ruler on a table so that the end of the ruler with the string tied to it hangs over the edge of the table. Place a few books on the other end of the ruler to hold it in place. The string with the weight will hang down to the floor.

3. Make the pendulum swing by pulling the rock to one side and letting it go again.

As the pendulum was set swinging, at what point along its path was the energy stored?

_____

_____

_____

What type of energy is being used—chemical, or mechanical?

_____

Activity 2: Spool Toy

1. Thread a rubber band through the inside of a spool of thread. Put the short toothpick through the loop on one end of the rubber band to hold it in place.

2. Turn the spool over. Place a washer on the spool so that the rubber band can be pulled through the center. Place the long toothpick through the other loop of the rubber band.

3. Place the toy on a flat surface so that the short toothpick is on the bottom. Using the long toothpick, turn the rubber band five times. When you let go, watch what happens to the spool toy.

4. Repeat Step 3 a few more times. With each test, change the number of times you turn the rubber band.

What happened when you let go of the toothpick?

_____

_____

Where was the energy stored?

_____

Activity 3: Chemical Changes

1. Take a piece of steel wool about the size of a quarter and place it around the bulb of the thermometer (so the steel wool touches the bulb). After five minutes, record the temperature shown on the thermometer. This is the starting temperature of the steel wool.

2. Place the steel wool in the cup and pour enough vinegar out of the steel wool and place it again around the bulb of the thermometer.

3. After five minutes, squeeze the excess vinegar out of the steel wool and place it again around the bulb of the thermometer. Place plastic wrap around the steel wool and secure it with a rubber band.

4. Watch the thermometer for a few minutes and record the highest temperature reading.

Starting temperature of the steel wool

_____

Highest temperature of the steel wool after another 5 minutes

_____

What happened to the temperature of the steel wool after it was in the vinegar?

_____

_____

A chemical change occurs as the vinegar reacts with the iron in the steel wool. The chemical change releases energy. What form of energy results from this release?

_____

_____

Name _____   Date _____

Assignment

Light and Sound Waves

You will be creating light and sound waves using a string or slinky. Follow the steps listed here to complete your assignment.

Materials:

- 8 to 10 feet of rope
- Slinky®
- masking tape

Part 1: Light Waves

1. Put a piece of masking tape around the middle of the rope. For this part, the tape will help you see the motion of particles <u>in</u> the wave.

2. Find a partner to hold one end of the rope or tie it to the leg of a table or chair.

3. Stretch out the rope but don't make it too tight. Be sure the rope is not touching the floor.

4. Move your arm in an up and down motion. In what direction does the wave move?

   _____

   _____

5. Move your arm faster. Describe the pattern of the waves formed in terms of amplitude and wavelength.

   _____

   _____

6. Move your arm up and down higher and lower. Describe the pattern of the waves formed in terms of amplitude and wavelength.

   _____

   _____

Summary: In a transverse wave, the particles of the wave move perpendicular to the direction of the wave (energy of the wave). Light is an example of a transverse wave.

Part 2: Sound Waves

7. Put a piece of masking tape around one wire in the middle of the Slinky®. In this part, the masking tape represents an air particle.

8. Find a partner to hold one end of the Slinky® or secure the Slinky® to the leg of a table or chair.

9. Stretch the Slinky® out. (Caution: Do not overstretch the Slinky®.)

10. Quickly push the Slinky® once toward your partner and then pull back. What direction did the wave move?

_____

_____

11. What did you observe about the movement of the tape in the middle of the Slinky®? What caused the tape (air particle) to move?

_____

_____

12. Draw a diagram of the wave traveling through the Slinky®. Label the direction the wave and the particle are moving.

Summary: In a longitudinal wave, the particles move in the same direction as the wave. Sound is an example of a longitudinal wave.

Student Guide

Energy Conversions

Think about the different types of energy you use every day. Does energy stay in the place and form in which it starts, or does it change? Learn about many ways that energy can transfer from one place to another or change from one form to another.

Lesson Objectives

- Recognize that energy can transfer from one place to another or convert from one form into another.
- Identify when a transfer of energy from one place to another or a conversion of energy from one form to another has taken place.
- Recognize that both machines and living things convert energy from one form into another, such as chemical energy into heat energy, light energy, or mechanical energy.
- Make observations to provide evidence that energy can be transferred from place to place by sound, light, heat, and electric currents.
- Generate or compare multiple solutions that use patterns to transfer information.

PREPARE

Approximate time is 60 minutes.

Materials

For the Student

    Baseball Energy
    Energy Transfer Assignment
    Comparing Analog and Digital Signals
    A Cabin for Mr. Potts
    glass jar
    graph paper
    pencil
    pen
    sand
    thermometer

Keywords and Pronunciations

conduction: The transfer of heat between two objects that are touching

convert: To change from one form to another. The chemical energy in gasoline is converted in a car's engine to heat energy, then to mechanical energy, making the car move.

efficiency: The amount of useful energy that is transferred

radiation: The transfer of energy by waves

transfer: To pass from one thing or place to another. When a pan is on a hot burner, heat energy is being transferred from the burner to the pan. The food in the pan is then cooked.

LEARN

Activity 1: Energy Changes *(Online)*

Activity 2: Labeling Forms of Energy *(Offline)*

Activity 3: Energy Transfers *(Online and Offline)*

Activity 4: Using Waves to Move Information *(Online and Offline)*

Activity 5: A House Full of Energy *(Offline)*

ASSESS

Lesson Assessment: Energy Conversions *(Offline)*

You will complete an offline assessment covering the main objectives of this lesson. Your learning coach will score this assessment.

Name _____   Date _____

Energy Conversions

Baseball Energy

Energy is being transferred and converted into other forms all around you.
Review some ways that this happens by playing a little baseball.

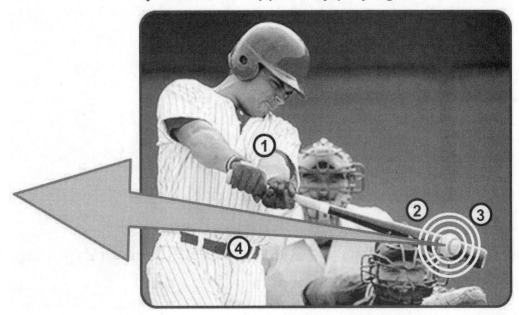

Look at the photo of the baseball player. Explain what is happening to the energy
at each numbered point. Be sure to describe what form of energy is used, and
how it is transferred or converted, including being stored. You may look back at
the last screen of the Explore section if you need to.

1. _____

   _____

2. _____

   _____

3. _____

   _____

4. _____

   _____

Name _____   Date _____

Assignment

Energy Transfer

In this activity, you trace the path as chemical energy is converted to heat energy.

Materials

- jar
- sand
- thermometer

Heat Transfer

1. Fill a small jar half full of sand.

2. Measure and record the initial temperature of the sand.

    Initial temperature: _____

3. Put a lid on the container and shake the sand vigorously for about 2 minutes.

4. Immediately measure and record the temperature of the sand.

    Final temperature: _____

5. Complete the Energy Transfer Diagram below:

    Chemical energy (from food you ate) → _____ Energy →

    _____ Energy.

6. The jar in your hand feels warm to your touch. What kind (conduction or radiant) of heat transfer is this?

    _____

    _____

When you are finished with your investigation, discuss your answers with your learning coach.

Name _____   Date _____

Assignment
Comparing Analog and Digital Signals

In this activity, you will compare analog and digital signals as a way to send information.

Materials

- pencil
- paper – five sheets
- graph paper – five sheets

Analog

1. Using a pencil, mark this paper as #1.

2. Put a second sheet of paper on top of your drawing and make a copy of it by tracing it. You may not erase if your pencil strays off the original line. Mark this paper as #2. Repeat and number so you have at least four copies. If you have family members available, have them make a copy!

3. Compare your last copy to the original drawing.

Digital

4. Make a simple drawing of a stick figure on the graph paper. But instead of drawing a line, make your stick figure by shading in the boxes of the graph paper.

5. Repeat Step 2, marking each copy #2–5.

6. Compare your last copy to the original drawing.

Think about

- Which drawing is closest to your original drawing? Why is it more accurate?
- Do you think analog or digital signals would be better for sending an image to another phone?

Summary

The analog signal is less accurate because the pencil line can vary. These differences are amplified the more you copy your drawing. The digital drawing should be identical because having only two options—filled or unfilled graph square—means less errors.

When you are finished with your investigation, discuss your answers with your learning coach.

Name _____ Date _____

Energy Conversions
A Cabin for Mr. Potts

As he turned the stove on to **scramble some eggs**, it occurred to Mr. Potts that everything he would do today came down to energy. Here he was, making breakfast to give him strength for what was ahead. And how did the energy get in his scrambled eggs? Why, **the chicken put it there**. How did the chicken get it? From eating seed. How did the seed get it? From the big old sun—and there it was now, just popping up over the horizon. Mr. Potts finished eating, washed his dishes under hot water—he liked it really hot—then started up his truck and drove off.

An hour later he was almost at his destination . . . but what on Earth? Mr. Potts stopped when he saw the crowd of people. It was ten of his friends, sipping hot coffee and leaning up against their cars! Loud music was coming from one of the car radios, an old song Mr. Potts loved. But what were they all doing here—here, in the place where he and his son had spent all year building a log cabin?

"Well, you guys chopped down the trees by yourselves, and you sawed them into logs by yourselves, and you made them into walls by yourselves," his friend Nancy said, seeing Mr. Potts climb out of his truck and coming over to shake his hand.

"Your family even grew the trees," her husband Mike added. "You guys never run out of energy." Everyone laughed. "But we aren't going to let you have all the fun—we're here to help put up the roof!"

Mr. Potts was amazed. He and his son Jim had been working on his special project—to build a log cabin—for nine months, and soon it would be finished. And there was his son, now. But what was he fiddling with behind that pickup truck?

"Check it out, Dad," Jim grinned. "Anne and Jerry have a gas-powered winch on their pickup truck. It runs on this gas motor here. You and I have been lifting logs with our hands for months, and this baby will help us do the rest of the job in just a couple of hours more!"

All afternoon the group worked together. As the day warmed up, people got hot. The pile of jackets grew. People were even wiping the sweat off their foreheads. They took the last logs and sawed them down to the right lengths. Some used chainsaws that ran on gas. Some used hand saws. Everyone pitched in. They climbed up on top of his cabin and nailed the pieces in tight. Some of his friends had brought their power nailers, which used batteries. Other friends used hammers. They even helped finish off the very top of the brick chimney. When Mr. Potts banged the last nail in everyone cheered. Especially Mr. Potts, who hadn't expected all that help to finish that very day.

"I'm glad the work's finished," Nancy said, "Because I haven't eaten a thing since breakfast. And now that we've stopped working, I'm noticing that it's starting to get a little cold out here."

"The way my dad works, I figured we'd miss lunch. So I wrapped up some food and put it in the car," Jim smiled. "Lots of nutritious stuff. All we need is a fireplace to stay warm."

"I know just the one," Mr. Potts said.

It was kind of a small cabin for 12 people to be in all at once. But they left the pile of jackets where it was. They started a fire, and crowded around it to eat, enjoying the results of their work. Mr. Potts, with a warm smile, thanked his friends.

Create a Table

Use the information from the story to create a table. Write down the activity, describe the conversion or transfer of energy, and identify whether the energy is from a living thing. A sample table has been created.

Activity	Energy Conversion or Transfer	Energy in Living Things
Example: Scramble eggs	Heat energy from the stove → chemical energy in cooked eggs	
Example: Chicken producing eggs	Chemical energy in food (seeds) →chemical energy in the chicken's body → chemical energy in egg cells	X

Student Guide
Conductors and Insulators

Energy can be carried from one place to another. It can even pass through solid objects. In this lesson we focus on heat energy. Some substances allow heat energy to pass through them quite easily, while others do not. Experiment with some objects to see how easily heat energy passes through them.

Lesson Objectives

- Compare the conduction of heat energy through different types of solids and determine which types are most effective in conducting heat energy.
- Explain how heat energy is conducted through a solid.
- Explain the difference between a thermal conductor and a thermal insulator.

PREPARE

Approximate lesson time is 60 minutes.

Materials

For the Student

    Drippy Spoon

Keywords and Pronunciation

thermal conduction: The passing of heat energy through a solid, liquid, or gas by collisions of molecules. When I touched the hot water pipe, thermal conduction allowed me to feel heat energy from the hot water inside.

thermal conductor: A material that allows heat energy to pass through it easily by collisions of its molecules. Since the hot water pipe was so warm on the outside, I knew it was made of a thermal conductor.

thermal insulator: A material that does not allow heat energy to pass through it easily by collisions of its molecules. I thought that we could keep the heat energy in the water better if we put a thermal insulator around the hot water pipe.

LEARN

Activity 1: Pass the Energy, Conductor *(Online)*

Activity 2: Drippy Spoon *(Offline)*

Safety

Use extreme caution when working with boiling water. Never leave your student unattended near hot or boiling water.

ASSESS

Lesson Assessment: Conductors and Insulators *(Offline)*

Sit with an adult to review the assessment questions.

Name _____   Date _____

Conductors and Insulators

Drippy Spoon

Test three types of materials (metal, plastic, and wood) to find out which conducts heat energy the best and which are good insulators. To do this, you will need a bowl of hot water, three pats of butter, and three spoons of equal size. One spoon should be made of metal, one of plastic, and one of wood.

Which do you predict will melt fastest when hot water is added to the bowl? The butter in the: metal spoon, plastic spoon, wooden spoon

_____

Which do you predict will melt slowest when hot water is added to the bowl? The butter in the: metal spoon, plastic spoon, wooden spoon

_____

Which material(s) do you predict will be the best thermal conductor(s)? metal, plastic, wood

_____

Which material(s) do you predict will be the best thermal insulators(s)? metal, plastic, wood

_____

To perform the experiment, complete the following steps.

1. Cut four small, equal-sized pieces of butter.

2. Lean the three spoons against the side of the bowl so they are standing up, as shown in the drawing on page 1.

3. Place a pat of butter on the bowl of each spoon. Make sure you put the butter at the same height from the bottom of each spoon.

4. Fill the bowl half way with hot water, making sure the water does not touch the butter.

5. Observe the pats of butter and note which one melts the fastest.

Which pat of butter melted the fastest?

_____

What happened to the pats of butter on the other spoons?

_____

_____

Were your predictions correct?

_____

Which material was the best conductor? Why?

_____

_____

Which materials were the best insulators?

_____

_____

In your own words, describe how the heat energy from the water was conducted from one end of the spoon to the other.

_____

_____

_____

_____

_____

Extension:

For a challenge, try this experiment:

1. Wrap a second, identical metal spoon with electrical tape.

2. Clean and cool off the metal spoon from the first experiment.

3. Repeat steps 1-5 from the first experiment, but this time only use the two metal spoons.

On which spoon did the butter melt faster this time?

_____

Both spoons are metal. Why did the tape keep the butter from melting as fast?

_____

_____

Did the tape act as a conductor or insulator?

_____

Student Guide
Energy Resources

You've learned a great deal about energy. Now discover the different resources that provide or release it. The different types are classified either as *renewable resources* or as *nonrenewable resources*. Let's learn more about them.

Lesson Objectives

- Describe the difference between a renewable and a non-renewable resource.
- Describe the use of a renewable resource.
- Identify renewable resources such as wood, sun, wind, or water, and non-renewable resources such as coal, natural gas, and oil.

PREPARE

Approximate lesson time is 60 minutes.

Advance Preparation

- You will need an egg carton for this science activity; a styrofoam egg carton is preferable. Cut the egg carton apart to make 12 small buckets. If your egg carton is not made of styrofoam, use plastic wrap to cover each bucket. Push the plastic wrap into the middle of each bucket so that it can be filled with water. In addition, you will need a sink to put the water wheel under a running tap while watching it lift the weight up.

Keywords and Pronunciation

nonrenewable resource: a resource that cannot be replenished in a short period of time

renewable resource: A resource that is produced at least as fast as it is used up. Wood is considered a renewable resource because we can grow more trees as fast as they are being used.

LEARN

Activity 1: Energy Sources *(Online)*

Activity 2: Which Energy Source Is Best? *(Offline)*

Activity 3: Water Wheel *(Offline)*

Instructions

Overview

Water wheels have been used for hundreds of years. They use the mechanical energy of moving or falling water to do work. In this activity, your student will build her own water wheel and watch how it lifts up a weight. She will need your help in putting it together.

Activity Steps

1. Cut two circles out of poster board 8 in. in diameter to use as wheels. Use plastic wrap to cover both wheels to make them waterproof.

2. Lay the wheels on top of each other and use a pencil to poke through the center of each circle. The pencil will act as the axle of the wheel.

3. If you have not already done so, cut up an egg carton to make 12 small buckets. Cover them with plastic wrap to make them waterproof.

4. Push the plastic wrap inside the buckets so that they will still catch water. Staple the buckets to the insides of the wheels to make the water wheel. Make sure that all the buckets face one way around the wheel, so that the water can fill them as the wheel rotates. See photo.

5. Tie two pieces of string to the pencil passing through the center of the water wheel. Tie the other ends of the string to a ruler so that, once tied, the wheel will hang down from the ruler.

6. With another piece of string, tie a second pencil to the first pencil, with the string tight on both. This will act as a weight that the water wheel will lift as it winds the string around the pencil that serves as an axle.

7. Put the wheel under a running tap and watch it lift the weight up.

ASSESS

Lesson Assessment: Energy Resources *(Offline)*

You will complete an offline assessment covering the main objectives of this lesson. Your learning coach will score this assessment.

LEARN

Activity 4: Solar Cooker *(Offline)*

Instructions

Overview

Did you know that heat from the sun could cook hot dogs just like a campfire? Build a solar cooker of your own and watch how the temperature rises.

Activity Steps

8. Line the inside of a shoebox lid with some aluminum foil.

9. Place a thermometer in the lid and place it in the sunlight. Write the temperature down in your science journal.

10. Wait ten minutes, and then record the temperature again. Move the lid into the shade and make the next part of the solar cooker.

11. Cut a piece of poster board into a rectangle 10 cm by 30 cm. Cover it with aluminum foil.

12. Use scissors to poke a hole about two cm from each end of the rectangle. Tie one end of a piece of string through one of the holes.

13. Pull the piece of string until the ends of the rectangle are 20 cm apart. This should make the rectangle bend, or bow. This will be the reflector piece of the solar cooker.

14. Move the cooker back into the sunlight. Put the reflector in the shoebox lid with the thermometer between the two ends of the rectangle.

15. Record the temperature. Leave the solar cooker in the sun for another ten minutes, and then record the temperature again.

Extension

How could you make the temperature rise even higher? Discuss ideas with your learning coach. After the discussion, design a new solar cooker that will raise the temperature in the solar cooker even more. Build your design and test it. What are the results? How could you improve upon your design? With your learning coach, make changes to your design to improve the solar cooker's ability to reach a higher temperature.

Student Guide

Energy: Unit Review and Assessment

Review what you have learned about energy and demonstrate your Energy Whiz talent. Then you will be ready to take the Energy Unit Assessment.

Lesson Objectives

- Demonstrate mastery of the skills taught in this unit.
- Identify different forms of energy, such as light energy, heat energy, and mechanical energy.
- Recognize that energy is neither created nor destroyed.
- Recognize that energy is the ability to cause change in structure or motion.
- Explain how heat energy is conducted through a solid.
- Explain the difference between a thermal conductor and a thermal insulator.
- Identify renewable resources such as wood, sun, wind, or water, and non-renewable resources such as coal, natural gas, and oil.
- Identify the Earth's major source of energy as the sun.
- Identify when a transfer of energy from one place to another or a conversion of energy from one form to another has taken place.
- Recognize that both machines and living things convert energy from one form into another, such as chemical energy into heat energy, light energy, or mechanical energy.
- Recognize that energy can be stored for later use in many forms, such as in food, fuel, batteries, and stretched rubber bands.
- Recognize that energy from the sun makes life on Earth possible.

PREPARE

Approximate lesson time is 60 minutes.

Materials

For the Student

Energy Scavenger Hunt

LEARN

Activity 1: Are You an Energy Whiz? *(Online)*

Activity 2: Energy Scavenger Hunt *(Offline)*

ASSESS

Unit Assessment: Energy *(Offline)*

Complete an offline Unit Assessment. Your learning coach will score the assessment.

Name _____   Date _____

Energy: Unit Review and Assessment
Energy Scavenger Hunt

Take an Energy Tour around your house to find the following items.

1. The sun is Earth's major source of energy. Solar energy makes life on Earth possible. Look out your window and list three things that are benefiting from the sun's energy.

_____

_____

_____

2. Energy is neither created nor destroyed. It comes in many forms such as *light energy*, *heat energy*, or *mechanical energy*. Look around your house and find at least one example of each of these three types of energy.

_____

_____

_____

3. Energy can be stored in many forms. Find at least three examples of where energy is stored for later use.

_____

_____

_____

4. Energy can be converted from one form to another. Give two examples of things in your house that are converting mechanical energy into sound energy.

_____

_____

5. Some objects are good thermal conductors, which means that they allow heat energy to pass through them easily by collisions of their molecules. Name three things in your house that are good thermal conductors.

_____

_____

_____

6. Thermal insulators allow little or no heat energy to pass through them by collisions of molecules. Name two objects from your house that are good thermal insulators.

_____

_____

7. Resources can be either renewable or non-renewable. List at least two examples of each type of resource.

_____

_____

Student Guide

Electric Charges and Magnetic Poles

All of us have had contact with electricity. We come into a room and turn on a light. We use a flashlight. We see lightning bolts. We also have experience with magnetism—our refrigerators stay closed using magnets, and many motors are loaded with them. Learn how these two things—electricity and magnetism—are related.

You already know something about electricity—just turn on a light! No doubt you have played with magnets, too, and have picked up metal objects with them. But did you know that electricity and magnetism are related?

Lesson Objectives

- Recognize that objects with the same electrical charges repel and objects with different electrical charges attract.
- Describe the Earth's magnetic field and identify magnetic north and south.

PREPARE

Approximate lesson time is 60 minutes.

Materials

For the Student

> Electric Discoveries: Your Scientist Notebook
> Come Here! Go Away!
> bar magnets, pair
> fabric, wool cloth
> household item - clothes hanger
> balloon (2)
> string

Keywords and Pronunciation

atom: A tiny particle that is the fundamental building block of any substance. The properties of an atom determine the properties of an element made up of only those atoms.

electron: A tiny part of an atom with a negative electrical charge. In an atom, electrons form a cloud around the nucleus.

proton: A tiny part of the nucleus of an atom, which has a positive electrical charge. The number of protons determines the chemical properties of the atom.

LEARN

Activity 1: Opposites Attract *(Online)*

Activity 2: Electric Discoveries: Your Scientist Notebook *(Offline)*

Keep a Scientist Notebook of electricity facts and fun you discover, just like famous scientists do.

Activity 3: Come Here! Go Away! *(Offline)*

Things are forced together, or *attract,* when their electrical charges are different. Things are pushed away, or *repel,* when their electrical charges are the same. Demonstrate these shocking events.

Safety

Do not use magnets near the computer.

ASSESS

Lesson Assessment: Electric Charges and Magnetic Poles *(Online)*

You will complete an online assessment covering the main objectives of this lesson. Your assessment will be scored by the computer.

Name _____   Date _____

Electric Charges and Magnetic Poles
Electric Discoveries: Your Scientist Notebook

How important is it to keep records? Think about important scientific discoveries and inventions. What if no one kept careful records of the movements of planets? What if no one kept notes on different kinds of complex treatments for diseases? Good written records help scientists remember exactly what they did, and what happened, without change. They can compare new experiments and results with old ones, and look for important differences and patterns.

Later in this unit you will learn about an English scientist named Michael Faraday. Michael Faraday made important discoveries in magnetism and electricity. He found that when a magnetic field increases or decreases, it produces electricity—an important principle used to build motors and generators.

This fine scientist began life with very little schooling as the son of a blacksmith. He loved books, so he worked in a bookbinder's shop. This job gave him the chance to read many books including encyclopedias and science books, as well as stories. He loved how he could check what he read in a chemistry book by doing his own observations, and so, personally, found the facts to be true.

Faraday was so interested in chemistry, that one day he borrowed money from a brother to attend a series of lectures on chemistry. These lectures had been created to teach young men just like him—not well off, but interested in science. He enjoyed these lectures on science so much, that he decided to become a "natural philosopher" (scientist). Since he had taken very careful records of the lectures he attended, he used his skills to bind them into a wonderful book. Then he presented the book to the director of the science institute that had offered the lectures, and asked for a job. Faraday was hired as a general assistant and bottle-washer: his first job close to science! While doing these tasks, he took time to document his own remarkable experiments, including the invention of the electric motor in 1821. He eventually became the director of that very institute where he first heard science lectures.

Faraday's story shows many reasons why taking notes and keeping records are important: he used his notes and records to show others what he had done, and what he was capable of doing. During the entire unit, you will keep a science record book of the electricity and magnetism activities and experiments you perform.

Section off a part of your science binder or staple special pages together so that you can take notes as Faraday did. Then write the title, "Electric Discoveries: My Scientist Notebook." After each activity in this unit, you will be prompted to write in your Scientist Notebook. After recording your thoughts throughout the next six lessons, you will compile and present your findings in your own science lecture.

Name _____ Date _____

Electric Charges and Magnetic Poles
Come Here! Go Away!

Rubbing two neutral objects causes electrons to move off one object and onto another.

- A negatively charged object has more negatively charged particles (electrons).
- A positively charged object has less negatively charged particles (less electrons).

Materials

Balloons, 2

String

Wool cloth

Bar magnets

Attracting

1. Tie the balloon to string and hang it in a place you can reach. (You may want to suspend it from a coat hanger).

2. Hold the cloth near the balloon.

3. Nothing happens. Why? They are both neutral.

4. Rub the balloon quickly with the cloth. You are rubbing electrons off the cloth and onto the balloon right at this moment!

5. Hold the cloth near the balloon. Write what you observe.

_____

_____

_____

Draw the positive and negative charges on the balloon and cloth before and after you rubbed the balloon.

Key

+ means positive

− means negative

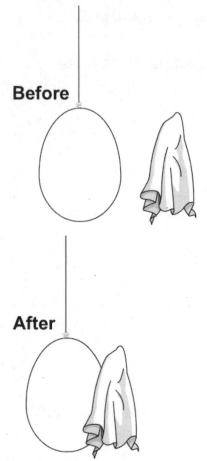

Before

After

Repelling

1. Tie a new balloon to string and hang it near the first balloon.

2. Rub both balloons with the cloth.

3. Place the balloons near each other. Write what you observe.

_____

_____

_____

Draw the charges on the balloons using the same key as before.

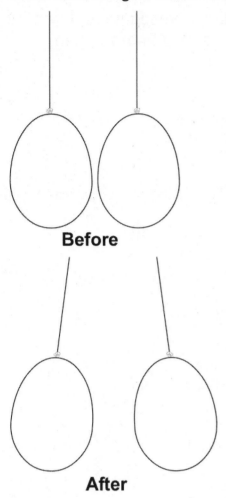

Before

After

Magnetism

Magnets have poles always in pairs that repel and attract. Investigate repelling and attracting with the magnets by placing their ends near each other. Then, label the poles in the illustrations.

Key

N = North pole

S = South pole

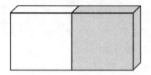 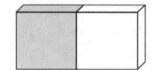

Repelling

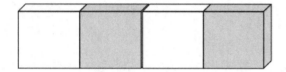

Attracting

Your Scientist Notebook

On a separate piece of paper, make your first electricity and magnetism entry in your Scientist Notebook. Write the date so you have a record of your notes. Then make careful entries for your balloon experiments and your magnet experiments. Imagine someone else was going to read your notes and try to do the same experiments you did, to see if they get the same results.

Do you need to repeat your experiments in different ways to make sure you know what is happening? Draw any diagrams you may need in order to explain your findings.

Student Guide
Magnet Madness

A magnet is a wonderful thing—especially when you start thinking about how it works. You know you can use a magnet to pick up many metal objects, but why? Explore how magnets work, and find out why scientists think the Earth acts like a giant magnet.

CAUTION: KEEP MAGNETS AWAY FROM YOUR COMPUTER.

Lesson Objectives

- Describe the Earth's magnetic field and identify magnetic north and south.
- Explain how to construct a temporary magnet.
- Explain that lightning is produced as a result of static discharge.

PREPARE

Approximate lesson time is 60 minutes.

Materials

For the Student

> Find Yourself
> bar magnets, pair
> household item - compass
> sewing needle
> bowl
> cardboard - float (foam, cork)
> water

Keywords and Pronunciation

atom: A tiny particle that is the fundamental building block of all substances. The properties of an atom determine the properties of an element made up only of those atoms.

aurora australis (uh-ROR-uh AW-struh-luhs)

aurora borealis (uh-ROR-uh bor-ee-A-luhs)**:** Lights seen at night in northern latitudes caused by electrically charged particles from the sun.

magnetic field: The magnetic effect every magnet creates in the space around it. The Earth has a very large magnetic field.

magnetic pole: A region of a magnet where the magnetic field is especially strong. All magnetic poles are either north or south poles. In a bar magnet, the poles are at the ends.

LEARN

Activity 1: Magnificent Magnets *(Online)*

Activity 2: Mapping with Magnets *(Offline)*

The world is a pretty big place, and if you don't know your way around you'll soon get lost. Make a temporary magnet and a tool that, for centuries, has been helping people find their way. Remember, stay far away from the computer when you work with magnets!

Activity 3: Scientist Notebook *(Offline)*

Today you made important "discoveries" about magnetism. As you know, it is important for scientists to keep records of their discoveries and investigations. Write about your discoveries in your notebook. Include the following:

- The date and time
- What you discovered as you made the compass and what you can use it for
- What happened to the needle as you magnetized it
- Any surprises that came up during the lesson

Make your notes clear enough that someone else finding them could do the same thing you did, and compare results with your results.

Use an index card to make a compass card. Write the north, south, east, and west on the card in their proper locations. Use your tool to find the following and record them in your notebook.

1. The direction the sun rises

2. The direction the sun sets

3. A building north of you

4. An organism south of you

5. Any object of your choice and its direction

Keep track of the entries you are making in your Scientist Notebook. You will need them at the end of the unit.

ASSESS

Lesson Assessment: Magnet Madness *(Offline)*

You will complete an offline assessment covering the main objectives of this lesson. Your learning coach will score this assessment.

Name _____ Date _____

Magnet Madness
Find Yourself

Exploring magnetism is fun, and so is using magnetism to explore! With a few simple tools, you can make a magnet that you can use as a compass. It's the same idea that ocean mariners and desert explorers have used for centuries.

A *compass* is a tool people use to figure out direction. It uses the Earth's magnetic north pole. Here's how it works:

- First, hold the compass in front of you. A compass has an N, S, W, and E for the four cardinal directions.
- Then, watch where the pointer stops.
- The pointer lines up with the Earth's magnetic field, with one side (the north side) attracted to the magnetic north pole.
- To align the compass, turn the compass body until the pointer is directly over the N. Label N on the paper.
- Once you know north, you can then figure out south, west, and east—or northeast or southwest or…

**This way
is north.**

Materials

needle

a float (cork, foam meat tray, cardboard)

bowl – not metal

water

bar magnet

tape

WARNING: Before working with magnets move far away from the computer. Use caution when working with the needle.

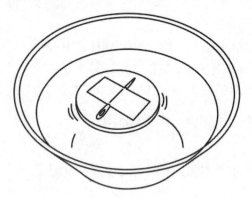

Procedure:

1. Fill the bowl with water to make your compass case. Glass or plastic bowls work best.

2. Make a float. A *float* is a small, flat piece of lightweight material that will float on water. Cardboard will work for a while, but cork or a piece of a foam meat tray is best.

3. Next, make a magnet. Put the needle flat on the bar magnet, with one end facing the N pole of the bar magnet, and the other facing the S pole. Now pull the needle by the end so it slides along its length from S pole to N pole, and repeat several times. Always pull in the same direction to keep from mixing up the magnetic poles.

4. Test your needle for magnetism—try sticking one end to the refrigerator or attracting other needles.

5. Once your needle is magnetized, attach it to the float with tape.

Troubleshooting:

- Other metals can interfere with your compass.
- If your container is too small or your float too large, your compass will be drawn to the side. Find a larger container.

1. Place your compass in the water with the needle side up. Let it settle down. What happens? Try turning the float around, and then gently turn the bowl.

_____

_____

_____

2. Explain how the needle became magnetic. Mention electrons in your answer.

_____

_____

_____

Student Guide

Static Electricity—Truly Shocking

It's a bit of shock to touch a doorknob and get...well...a shock. Why does this happen? Find out more about static electricity and learn how a charge is built up and how a charge is discharged.

Lesson Objectives

- Explain that friction can build up static electrical charges when two objects are rubbed together and transfer electrons from one surface to the other.
- Explain that lightning is produced as a result of static discharge.
- Recognize that *static electricity* is the buildup of electrical charges on an object.
- Recognize that *electric current* is the flow of electrons through a wire.

PREPARE

Approximate lesson time is 60 minutes.

Materials

For the Student

> Action Static
> household item - comb
> household item - puffed rice
> household item - wool sweater or cloth
> balloon
> water - (sink)
> Get a Charge from an Electroscope
> jar - glass
> index cards, 4" x 6"
> paper clip - large, uncoated

Keywords and Pronunciation

conduction: The application of an electric charge to an object by direct contact with a charged object. The glass rod got its electric charge by conduction.

friction: Rubbing two objects together to create an imbalance of charges. Friction was part of the reason I got shocked when I touched the doorknob.

induction: The application of an electric charge to an object through the nearness of a charged object. The glass globe got its electric charge by induction.

static electricity: Electricity on the surface of objects, better thought of as unbalanced-charge electricity. Lightning is the huge discharge of static electricity charge from a cloud.

LEARN

Activity 1: More Than Just a Shock *(Online)*

Activity 2: Action Static *(Offline)*

Understanding static electricity will help you understand what goes on behind the scenes of what may seem like tricks. See how static works in interesting ways, then make notes of what you see in your Scientist Notebook.

Activity 3: Electroscope *(Online)*

An electroscope is a cool tool for studying electricity. It works with conduction of charges from one object to another.

ASSESS

Lesson Assessment: Static Electricity—Truly Shocking *(Offline)*

You will complete an offline assessment covering the main objectives of this lesson. Your learning coach will score this assessment.

Name _____ Date _____

Static Electricity—Truly Shocking

Action Static

What are some examples of static electricity?

1. _____

2. _____

3. _____

One way to produce static electricity is with friction. When you rub two things together, friction causes electrons to move from one object to another. The object that gains electrons becomes negatively charged. The object that loses electrons becomes positively charged. With these unbalanced charges, you can observe interesting effects. Some people may believe they are tricks, but there's real science behind them that you should know.

Materials

wool sweater or cloth

balloon

puffed rice cereal

comb

water (sink)

Part 1: The Comb and Water Trick

1. Turn on a water faucet and allow a thin stream of water to flow.

2. Charge the comb by rubbing it many times with the wool cloth.

3. Hold the comb close to the stream.

Make notes about what you see happening in your Science Notebook.

Part 2: The Puffed Rice in a Balloon Trick

1. Put 5 to 10 pieces of puffed-rice cereal into a deflated balloon.

2. Inflate the balloon and tie it closed.

3. Hold the balloon with one hand so that the mouth of the balloon is against your body.

4. Charge the balloon by stroking it 20 to 25 times with the piece of wool cloth.

5. Hold the balloon by the mouth so it hangs down freely.

6. If needed, give the balloon a little thump to get the puffed rice to the bottom of the balloon.

7. Slowly move your finger toward the cereal until your finger touches the balloon.

8. Rub the palm of your hand over the entire lower part of the balloon.

Make notes in your Science Notebook about what you see happening. Think about what types of charges attract and repel. Make sure someone else could repeat what you did from reading your notes.

Part 3: Science Notebook

Consider what you saw today in your activities. In your Science Notebook, explain why they are not tricks. Tell what happened to the objects that made them behave the way they did. Note any surprises or unexplained phenomena. Did you try your own tests after these two? What did you notice then? Don't forget to date your notes.

Explain your notes to an adult to check your work.

Name _____   Date _____

Static Electricity—Truly Shocking

Get a Charge from an Electroscope

This time, take a backward approach to learn about a cool science tool. Make an electroscope first, try some tests, then see if you can figure out what happened.

Materials

balloon

paper clip – large

aluminum foil

tape

scissors

wool sweater or cloth

glass jar

index card

Procedure

1. Unfold the paper clip and stick it through an index card.

2. Refold the paper clip so it looks like an S.

3. Take a long, thin strip of aluminum foil and wrap the middle once or twice around the bottom part of the S. The two sides of the strip should be equal and should hang down, not touching but very close together.

4. Place the index card on the top of the jar and tape it to the rim. The foil strips should be inside the jar and the top of the paper clip should be outside. This is your electroscope.

5. Charge a balloon by rubbing it with a wool cloth in the same direction 25 to 30 times.

6. Bring the balloon close to the paper clip outside the jar.

What happened?

You should see the foil strips separate.

Why?

When you touch the charged balloon to the electroscope, negative charges are transferred to the wire. What type of static buildup occurs when one charged object touches another object?

_____

The buildup of negative charges travels down the wire to the foil strips. The strips are overloaded with negative charges. Lots of negative charges are lots of similar charges, and you know what happens to similar charges … they repel!

Science Notebook

Sketch and label an electroscope in your notebook. Draw a diagram showing how negative charges are transferred from the balloon to the wire, and then to the aluminum strips. Use plus signs for positive charges and minus signs for negative charges. Date your work.

Share your diagram with an adult to check your work.

Student Guide

Electric Currents

The electricity you are most familiar with is the kind that comes to your house through wires. How does this kind of electricity differ from static electricity? In what ways is it similar? Find out about electric currents and how electrons can flow through wires.

Lesson Objectives

- Differentiate between a series circuit and a parallel circuit.
- Identify the parts of a circuit: battery, light, wire, and switch.
- Recognize that electric current is the flow of electrons through a wire.
- State that electric currents flow easily through materials that are conductors and do not flow easily through materials that are insulators.
- Make observations to provide evidence that energy can be transferred from place to place by sound, light, heat, and electric currents.

PREPARE

Approximate time is 60 minutes.

Advance Preparation

- One site you may use to purchase the 4.5v battery is www.campmor.com. If you choose not to purchase one, 2 D size batteries will work for the experiment in lieu of the 4.5v battery. Make sure you place them with positive and negative ends facing each other.
- Save the completed circuit for use in the next lesson.

Materials

For the Student

> Build a Circuit Assignment
> electrical tape
> electrical wire, plastic coated - 2 feet
> light bulb holders (3)
> light bulbs, miniature (5)
> battery - 4.5 V (D cell can work)
> brads (2)
> cardboard
> knife
> paper clip
> scissors
> Make an Electric Quiz Board
> hole punch
> light bulb - small
> light bulb holder

Keywords and Pronunciations

electric current: The flow of electrons through a wire

LEARN

Activity 1: Electric Currents *(Online)*

Activity 2: Build a Circuit *(Offline)*

Investigate the flow of electric current by building two types of circuits. Remove parts of the circuits to see the effects.

Safety

The bulbs may be hot. Use a cloth or oven mitt to unscrew them.

ASSESS

Lesson Assessment: Electric Currents *(Offline)*

You will complete an offline assessment covering the main objectives of this lesson. Your learning coach will score this assessment.

LEARN

Activity 3: Optional: Make an Electric Quiz Board *(Offline)*

From what you've learned, you can build a quiz board that you can use with your friends. Test them on their electricity knowledge! Have your friends compete for prizes.

Name _____   Date _____

Assignment
Build a Circuit

How are parallel and series circuits different? Construct both types to investigate. ⟩
Record your observations in your Scientist Notebook.

Materials

- 4.5-volt battery
- small bulbs, 4
- bulb holders, 2
- paper clip
- electrical tape
- copper wire, 60 cm – cut into 4 pieces and strip the ends
- cardboard
- brass fasteners, 2
- scissors
- knife

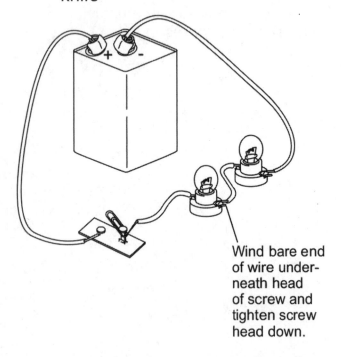

Wind bare end
of wire under-
neath head
of screw and
tighten screw
head down.

Lab Safety:

The bulbs may be hot. Use a cloth or oven mitt to unscrew them.

Procedure

1. Join the battery, bulbs, and wires in a series circuit as shown. Use electrical tape to attach the wires to the battery.

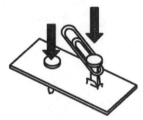

2. Push one paper fastener through cardboard. Hook a paper clip to the second fastener and push this fastener through the cardboard.

3. Turn the cardboard over. Wrap one wire around each paper fastener. Tape down the legs of the fastener.

4. Press the paper clip onto the free paper fastener. Electricity should flow.

Series circuit

Use your switch to turn the lights on. While both bulbs are lit, unscrew one of the bulbs.

Record your observations in your Scientist Notebook.

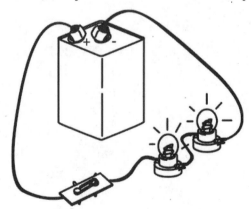

Parallel circuit

Set up a parallel circuit as shown. While both bulbs are lit, unscrew one of the bulbs. Record your observations in your Scientist Notebook.

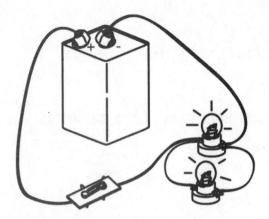

Scientist Notebook

Answer the following questions in your Scientist Notebook.

1. How do you know your circuits were complete?

2. Compare the brightness of the bulbs in the series circuit to the bulbs in the parallel circuit.

3. Compare the effect of unscrewing the bulbs in a series circuit to the bulbs in the parallel circuit.

4. How is the flow of electricity different in a series circuit and a parallel circuit?

5. Some older types of holiday lights would not work if even one bulb burned out. What kind of circuit was this? How were lights improved by changing the kind of circuit?

6. Why did the light bulbs feel hot after the circuit was turned on?

7. Using the drawing, show where the energy transformations occur between electric currents, heat, and light.

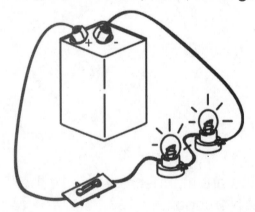

Share your answers with an adult to check them.

Name _____   Date _____

Electric Currents
Make an Electric Quiz Board

Have an adult help you follow the directions to make an electric quiz board that lights up when someone knows the right answer.

Materials

cardboard, sturdy – 33 cm tall x 30 cm wide

hole punch

light bulb

bulb holder

battery – D-cell or 4.5 volt

brass fasteners, 12

metal paper clips, 14

copper wire, 3 m

scissors

masking tape

electrical tape

crayons for decorating (optional)

Procedure

1. Punch six holes down each side of the cardboard, about 2 cm from the edges.

2. Slip a brass fastener through each hole and bend over the ends on the back.

3. Cut the wire into six 35 cm pieces, two 45 cm pieces, and one 17 cm piece. If the wire is insulated, strip the ends of insulation.

4. Wrap the bare end of each medium length wire to a paper clip so it makes a good contact. These wires will connect your questions and correct answer (or answers).

5. Use the longest wires for the front of the board. Add a paper clip to the end of each long wire. Connect the bare end of one wire to a D-cell battery with tape.

6. Connect the bare end of the other long wire to the bulb holder.

7. Use the shortest wire to connect the other end of the battery to the other bulb holder connection.

8. Write a multiple-choice question. Cut the question and the answers apart. Tape them next to a brass fastener "button" on the front of the board.

9. Hang one medium-sized connector paperclip on the question. Hang the other on the answer. Connect the two wires.

10. Test your quiz board. Touch one of the paper clips on the long wire to the question and the other paper clip on the long wire to the answer.

Does the light bulb light up? If not, check all your connections to see they are secure and try again. Double check all your questions and answers to see that you have wired them correctly. When you get it to work, can you explain what's making your Electric Quiz Board work?

Student Guide

Resistance, Conductors, Insulators

The materials that make up a circuit play an important part in the flow of electrical charges through a circuit. You will learn that a charge travels easier through some materials than others. For example, in some materials, electrical charges cannot flow at all. These materials can help make the use of electricity safer.

Lesson Objectives

- Describe how certain materials affect the flow of electricity through a wire.
- Give examples of conductors and insulators.
- State that electric currents flow easily through materials that are conductors and do not flow easily through materials that are insulators.

PREPARE

Approximate lesson time is 60 minutes.

Materials

For the Student

> Conductors and Insulators
> coin
> drinking glass
> household item - 2 ft - covered wire
> household item - 4.5 volt battery
> household item - bulb holder
> household item - small lightbulb
> plastic
> rubber band
> aluminum foil
> paper clip
> paper, notebook
> pencil
> tape, clear

Keywords and Pronunciation

conductor: Any material through which electricity can flow. A copper wire is a good conductor of electric charge as it flows through the circuit.

insulator: A substance that cannot conduct electricity very well. The rubber casing around the speaker wire serves as an insulator for the electrical current.

resistance: A measure of how strongly a substance opposes the flow of electricity. The unit of resistance in an electric circuit is the ohm.

LEARN

Activity 1: More About Circuits *(Online)*

Activity 2: Conductors and Insulators *(Offline)*

You already know how to create an electrical circuit using wire and a battery. Now add new materials to the circuit to see what effect they have on the bulb in the circuit. Will the bulb light up?

Caution: Bulbs may get hot.

Safety

Bulbs may get hot.

ASSESS

Lesson Assessment: Resistance, Conductors, Insulators *(Online)*

You will complete an online assessment covering the main objectives of this lesson. Your assessment will be scored by the computer.

Name _____   Date _____

Resistance, Conductors, Insulators

Conductors and Insulators

The circuit you created uses a battery, a copper wire, a switch, and a bulb. When the circuit is closed, the bulb will light up.

Hypothesis:

Using the same circuit, what do you predict will happen when you add any of the following materials as a part of the circuit?

Materials	Will the material complete the circuit and light the bulb?
Aluminum foil	
Drinking glass	
Paper clip	
Coin	
Pencil	
Paper	
Rubber band	

Materials:

completed circuit

aluminum foil

drinking glass

paper clip

coin

pencil

paper

rubber band

Lab Safety:

Do not touch the bulbs. They may be hot.

Procedure:

1. Remove the switch from the circuit. Do not attach the two ends of wire.

2. Place a piece of aluminum foil between the two ends of wire. Touch both ends of the wire to the aluminum foil.

3. Does this action complete the circuit and light the bulb? Record your observations in the table below.

4. Repeat the procedure using the remaining items in the table instead of aluminum foil.

Observations/Analysis:

Materials	Did the material complete the circuit and light the bulb?
Aluminum foil	
Drinking glass	
Paper clip	
Coin	
Pencil	
Paper	
Rubber band	

Science Notebook:

What conclusions can you draw about the materials that completed the circuit and lit the bulb? What about the materials that did not light the bulb?

_____

_____

_____

_____

Student Guide

Electromagnetism

In this lesson you will learn more about the relationship between electricity and magnetism. You will also see how a doorbell works and understand electric generators and motors.

KEEP MAGNETS AWAY FROM COMPUTER AT ALL TIMES.

Lesson Objectives

- Describe how to increase or decrease the strength of an electromagnet.
- Recognize that electromagnets are used in electric motors, generators, and other devices, such as doorbells and earphones.
- State that electric current produces magnetic fields and that an electromagnet can be made by wrapping a wire around a piece of iron and then running electricity through the wire.

PREPARE

Approximate lesson time is 60 minutes.

Advance Preparation

- You will need to save your copper wire for the electromagnet investigation in this lesson.
- One site you may use to purchase the 4.5v battery is www.campmor.com. If you choose not to purchase one, 2 D size batteries will work for the experiment in lieu of the 4.5v battery. Make sure you place them with positive and negative ends facing each other.

Materials

For the Student

    The Strongest Electromagnet
    battery - 4.5 volt
    copper wire
    nail, iron - not rusty
    paper clip - 20

Keywords and Pronunciation

electromagnet: A temporary magnet made using electric current, usually running around a metal core.

Hans Christian Oersted (hahns KREES-tyahn OUR-sted)

LEARN

Activity 1: Electromagnetism *(Online)*

Activity 2: The Strongest Electromagnet *(Offline)*

Annabelle and Simon were two students who decided to make an electromagnet. They found that one electromagnet was stronger than the other. Why were their electromagnets so different if they were made the same way? Make an electromagnet to find out.

Safety

Move well away from the computer and any wet area before doing this experiment.

Wear safety gloves when handling wires through which the current is flowing. Thick or electrical safety gloves are suggested.

ASSESS

Lesson Assessment: Electromagnetism *(Offline)*

You will complete an offline assessment covering the main objectives of this lesson. Your learning coach will score this assessment.

Name _____ Date _____

Electromagnetism
The Strongest Electromagnet

The circuit you created uses a battery, a copper wire, a switch, and a bulb. When the circuit is closed, the bulb will light up.

Using wire, an iron core, and a battery to make an electromagnet is a simple way to see the relationship between electricity and magnetism. Some electromagnets are stronger than others. Investigate two ways you can change the strength of an electromagnet.

The Story:

Annabelle and Simon had just learned about electromagnets. They both decided to build electromagnets to see who could make the strongest one.

They both found clean iron nails, not rusty old ones. They both wrapped their nails with copper wire, in tight coils. They both attached one end of the wire to the positive end of a 4.5 volt battery and the other end of the wire to the negative end. Then, Annabelle and Simon attempted to pick up paper clips with their electromagnets.

Annabelle's electromagnet picked up more paper clips than Simon's. Her electromagnet was stronger. They examined both electromagnets to see what could have made the difference. After observing the two magnets for a while they had an idea. They tried their idea in a new experiment. They wanted to find out if wrapping the wire more times around the nail made an electromagnet stronger.

Hypothesis:

Predict whether or not more coils will make an electromagnet stronger. Give a reason for your prediction.

_____

_____

_____

Materials

battery – 4.5 volt

iron nail – not rusty

paper clips – about 20

copper wire

bar magnet

Procedure:

1. Wrap the iron nail with the copper wire 10 times. Make your coils tight.

2. Attach one end of the wire to the positive end of the battery. Attach the other end to the negative end.

3. Hold your electromagnet over a pile of paper clips and try to pick some up.

4. Repeat steps 1 through 3 two more times making 20 coils and then 30 coils.

Circle what you change in the experiment (independent variable). Underline what will happen because of the change (dependent variable).

kind of nail	number of coils	strength of magnetism
voltage of battery	kind of wire	kind of paper clips

Observations

Number of coils	Number of paper clips
10	
20	
30	

Analysis

Make a bar graph to show how the strength of the electromagnet changed during each try.

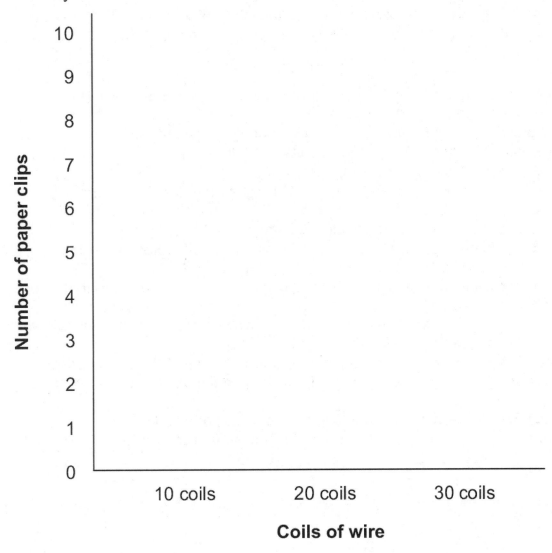

Conclusion

In your Scientist Notebook, describe the test you conducted today. Answer the question:

1. What is the likely reason that Annabelle's magnet was stronger? Can you think of another reason Annabelle's magnet might be stronger? Describe an experiment you might do to test that idea.

_____

_____

_____

Student Guide

Electricity and Magnetism: Unit Review and Assessment

Flip your light switch to "on" as you review the unit and take the Unit Assessment. Present all of the findings you made during your investigation of electricity and magnetism.

Lesson Objectives

- Demonstrate that magnets have two poles (north and south) and that like poles repel each other while unlike poles attract each other.
- Describe the earth's magnetic field and identify magnetic north and south.
- Differentiate between series and parallel circuits.
- Explain how to construct a temporary magnet.
- Explain that friction can build up static electrical charges when two objects are rubbed together and transfer electrons from one surface to the other.
- Identify the parts of a circuit: battery, light, wire, and switch.
- Recognize that electromagnets are used in electric motors, generators, and other devices, such as doorbells and earphones.
- Recognize that objects with the same electrical charges repel and objects with different electrical charges attract.
- State that electric currents flow easily through materials that are conductors and do not flow easily through materials that are insulators.
- State that electric currents produce magnetic fields and that an electromagnet can be made by wrapping a wire around a piece of iron and then running electricity through the wire.
- Describe the Earth's magnetic field and identify magnetic north and south.
- Demonstrate mastery of the important knowledge and skills of this unit.

PREPARE

Approximate lesson time is 60 minutes.

Materials

For the Student

> Posters and Presenting: Be a Modern-Day Faraday
> household item - assorted art supplies
> tape, adhesive
> cardboard - or posterboard
> markers
> paper, construction, 9" x 12"
> paper, notebook

LEARN

Activity 1: Electric Obstacle Course *(Online)*

Activity 2: Be a Modern Day Faraday *(Offline)*

Good scientists notice details about their experiments. Great scientists write them down. Even better scientists make a poster! Share some things you discovered while being a super scientist during this unit.

ASSESS

Unit Assessment: Electricity and Magnetism *(Offline)*

Complete an offline Unit Assessment. Your learning coach will score the assessment.

LEARN

Activity 3: Optional: ZlugQuest Measurement *(Online)*

Name _____ Date _____

Electricity and Magnetism:
Unit Review and Assessment
Posters and Presenting: Be a Modern-Day Faraday

During this unit on electricity and magnetism, you have been keeping notes in your scientist notebook. You started this after reading about Michael Faraday, an English scientist who kept careful notes about experiments because he knew it would help make him a smarter person.

Michael Faraday enjoyed sharing his notes with others. He always talked to his discussion group about electricity.

Share what you have learned about electricity and magnetism with an adult. Make a poster about what you have studied:

- Static
- Magnets
- Electric currents and circuits
- Conductors and insulators
- Electromagnets

On your poster, include a fact and picture about each topic in the list. You might even include something surprising you found out during your experiments. Use a large enough piece of paper or poster board (you can tape smaller pieces together). Write large so people can read your poster.

Give your presentation a catchy title. When you present your poster, be sure to tell WHAT you studied, WHEN, and HOW. Tell where people can get in touch with you after your presentation.

Student Guide
Rocks and Minerals

A simple rock might not look like much. Look closer, however, and you will see that it is formed from smaller substances—minerals. Where do minerals come from? What are they made of? Discover the answers to these questions, and learn how the birth of rocks is related to two awesome phenomena in nature—volcanoes and earthquakes.

Minerals and rocks are only part of the materials that make up the Earth. From its solid metallic core to the pebbles scattered on a beach, the Earth is a complex mixture of layers and materials.

Lesson Objectives

- Explain that rock is composed of different combinations of minerals.
- Identify the four main layers of the Earth and describe their characteristics.

PREPARE

Approximate lesson time is 60 minutes.

Advance Preparation

- In this Science activity, your student will be using the rock kit for the first time. For the first few lessons in this unit she should not know the identity of the different rocks and minerals. Remove the lid with the key from the box, and set it aside for later reference.

Materials

For the Student

> Rock Samples
> K12 Rocks and Minerals Kit
> magnifying glass
> paper, notebook
> pencil

Keywords and Pronunciation

Andriji Mohorovicic (ahn-DREE-yah maw-hawr-oh-VEE-chech)

crust: Earth's hard, rocky covering. The crust is the outermost layer of the Earth.

crystal: A solid substance whose atoms are arranged in repeating patterns. Crystals can be very beautiful, often looking like jewels.

galena (guh-LEE-nuh)

igneous (IG-nee-uhs): A class of rocks that forms from magma and lava. Obsidian may look like black glass but, in fact, it is a kind of igneous rock.

inner core: The center of Earth. Scientists think it is made of solid iron and nickel. The inner core has 30 times more mass than the moon.

mantle: the part of earth that is beneath the crust and is made up of rock; about 84 percent of the earth's volume is in the mantle

metamorphic (meh-tuh-MOR-fik)**:** A class of rocks that forms when heat and pressure act on igneous or sedimentary rock.

mineral: A nonliving substance that is made up of crystals and is found in nature. The Earth's crust contains many minerals.

outer core: The part of Earth that is beneath the mantle and contains melted iron and nickel. The outer core surrounds the inner core.

rock: A hard material made up of two or more minerals. There are three categories of rocks in the Earth.

LEARN

Activity 1: The Stuff of the Earth *(Online)*

Activity 2: Rock Sampling *(Offline)*

It's time to become a Rock Explorer! Look inside your rock kit to see samples of different rocks and minerals. Explore the samples and use a magnifying glass to find what characteristics they may have in common.

ASSESS

Lesson Assessment: Rocks and Minerals *(Offline)*

You will complete an offline assessment covering the main objectives of this lesson. Your learning coach will score this assessment.

LEARN

Activity 3: Optional: Nearby Rocks *(Online)*

Diamonds are found only in certain places around the world. Do you think there are diamonds near your house?

See what types of rocks and minerals are mined in your state.

You will be doing a web search to learn more. Web searches should always be done with adult supervision. K12 recommends the use of the safe search options that most web browsers come with, or one of the safe search engines produced by many major search engine providers.

Find more about this topic. Search for these key terms:

- minerals mined in each state

Safety

As always, you may wish to preview any websites before your student views them.

Name _____   Date _____

Rocks and Minerals

Rock Samples

Are you ready to explore your rock kit? It contains both rocks and minerals, and they all have different characteristics. Take some time to look at each sample. How does each one feel? What colors can you see? If you use a magnifying glass can you see any crystals?

Place all the samples on a table. Separate the dark samples from the light samples, and use the numbers on the rocks to fill in the chart below. Then re-classify the samples looking for the rest of the characteristics listed on the chart.

Characteristics	Rock Numbers
Dark in color	
Light in color	
Visible crystals	
No visible crystals	
Visibly different minerals	
No visibly different minerals	
No visibly different minerals with visible crystals	
No visibly different minerals with no visible crystals	

Student Guide

Crystal Shapes

Crystals are some of the most beautiful of nature's creations. The faint reflection from a ruby or emerald is a wonderful thing to behold. What are crystals, though, and why do they sparkle and gleam the way they do? You'll find that the arrangement of their atoms or molecules holds the key to understanding crystals.

Lesson Objectives

- Describe two types of crystal structures—cubic and hexagonal.
- Explain that the size of a crystal depends on the rate at which it was cooled.

PREPARE

Approximate lesson time is 60 minutes.

Advance Preparation

- In this science lesson, your student will be using the rock kit for the second time. For the first few lessons in this unit, we don't want her to know the identity of the different rocks and minerals. Remove the lid with the key from the box, and set it aside for later reference.
- Your student will need at least four days for crystals to grow in the "Cool" Crystals activity. Start the investigation early, or start it during the lesson and return to it later.

Materials

For the Student
    Crystal Shapes
    "Cool" Crystals
    jar - baby food/plastic cups (2)
    oven mitt
    salt - Epsom
    heat source
    magnifying glass
    pipe cleaners
    pot
    ruler
    safety goggles
    spoon
    water

Keywords and Pronunciation

crystal: A substance, often made of a single compound or element, that forms in a regular repeating pattern as rocks cool. I found a quartz crystal inside a granite rock.

cubic: A type of crystal structure formed from stacks of four-sided shapes (cubes). The crystal structure of gold is cubic.

hexagonal: A type of crystal structure formed from six-sided shapes. Ice has a hexagonal crystal structure.

LEARN

Activity 1: Amazing Crystals *(Online)*

Safety

As always, you may wish to preview any websites before your student views them.

Activity 2: Crystal Shapes *(Offline)*

Do you know what *orderly* means? A room with clothing folded and put away and trash emptied is orderly. Rocks contain orderly parts called *crystals.* Crystals form in regular patterns over and over again. Explore two types of crystal patterns.

Activity 3: "Cool" Crystals *(Offline)*

Crystals form in different patterns but also in different sizes. Find out the effect of how fast a crystal cools on its size.

Note: Perform this activity with an adult. Wear safety goggles and use caution when handling hot objects.

Safety

Perform this activity with an adult. Wear safety goggles and use caution when handling hot objects.

ASSESS

Lesson Assessment: Crystal Shapes *(Offline)*

You will complete an offline assessment covering the main objectives of this lesson. Your learning coach will score this assessment.

Name _____ Date _____

Crystal Shapes

Rocks are made of two or more crystals. Each kind of crystal has its own special shape. The pattern of a crystal's shape is called a *lattice*. You've studied two kinds of lattices: cubic and hexagonal.

Fill in the name of the shape that stacks to create the pattern.

A cubic lattice is formed from stacked _____.

A hexagonal lattice is formed from stacked _____.

Procedure

1. Study the patterns. Color the faces of the patterns. The face is the part that will be on the outside after you fold the pattern.
2. Cut each pattern.
3. Fold each pattern on the lines.
4. Tape the tabs of each pattern together.

Observations

1. Check both shapes. Are all the faces showing on both crystals?

   _____

   _____

2. Study the following rocks from your kit: Rock 7, Rock 12, and Rock 13. Which appear to have a cubic lattice pattern? Which appear to have a hexagonal lattice pattern?

   _____

   _____

Investigation Idea

Ice has a hexagonal crystal structure. Observe ice for this pattern.

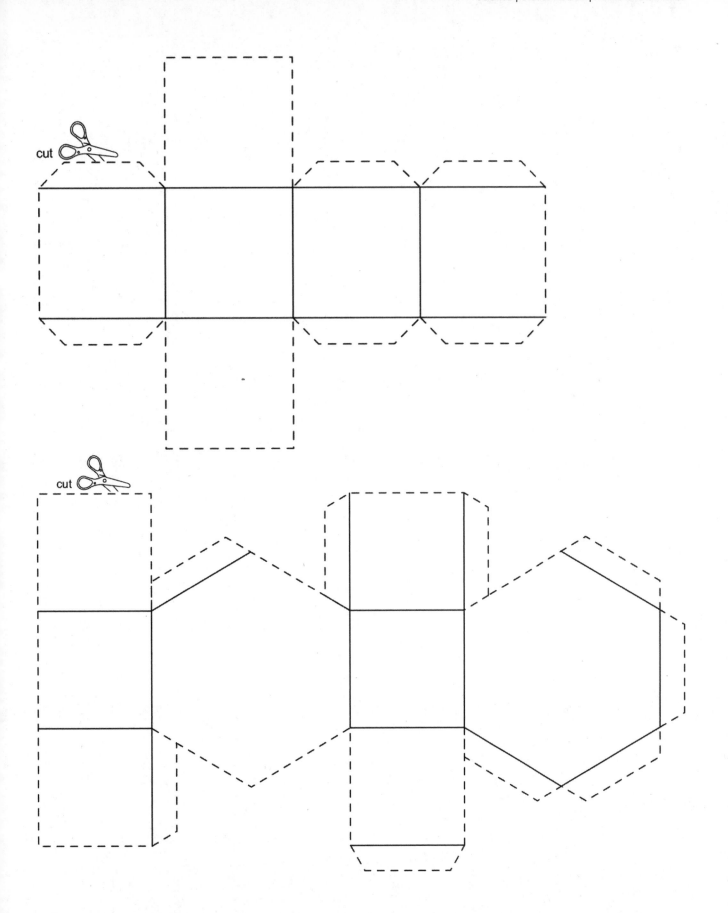

cut

cut

Name _____   Date _____

Crystal Shapes

"Cool" Crystals

If one crystal cools quickly and another cools slowly, will that have an effect on the size of the crystals? Crystals are formed deep within the Earth so it is necessary to use a model to investigate this question. Use salt crystals to find out the answer to this question.

Hypothesis:

Will quick cooling result in larger or smaller crystals? Write a hypothesis to answer this question. Do not use the words *I think*.

_____

_____

LAB SAFETY:

Perform this activity with an adult. Wear safety goggles and use caution when handling hot objects.

Materials

goggles

heat source

pot

oven mitts

water – 300 mL

Epsom salts - 600 mL

spoon

two baby food jars (or plastic cups)

pipe cleaners

magnifying lens

ruler

Procedure

1. Wrap two pipe cleaners around a pencil so that one end hangs down about 1 cm above the bottom of the jar.

2. Heat the water until it is near boiling.

3. Stir in Epsom salts until they are dissolved.

4. Fill the baby food jars half way with the solution.

5. Lay the pencil with the pipe cleaners on top of the jar so the pipe cleaner hangs down.

1. Place one jar in the refrigerator to cool and the other in a place in the room where it will not be disturbed.

2. Observe the crystals at the times listed in the chart. After 4 hours, use the ruler to measure the crystal sizes.

3. Record all data in the chart.

Scientist Notebook

Circle what you change in the experiment (independent variable). Underline what will happen because of the change (dependent variable).

Rate of cooling   Amount of water

Size of crystals   Height of pipe cleaner

Amount of salt   Color of pipe cleaner

Observations

Write your cup observations in the spaces on the chart. Record the size of the largest crystals after 4 days in the Measurement column.

Cup	Day 1	Day 2	Day 3	Day 4	Measurement
A					
B					

Analyze

1. In which jar did crystals form the fastest? The slowest?

_____

_____

2. In which jar did the smallest crystals form? The largest?

_____

_____

Conclusion

1. The crystals were cooled the fastest in the refrigerated jar. The crystals in the other jar cooled the slowest. What is the effect of how fast the crystals were cooled on their size?

_____

_____

2. Check the hypothesis you made. Did you prove it?

_____

_____

Investigation Idea

Repeat the experiment in this investigation with sugar, table salt, and rock salt. Compare their crystal shapes and sizes.

Student Guide

Properties of Minerals

The rocks that we see around us are built up of different kinds of minerals. Identifying minerals and learning about their properties are the first steps toward understanding rocks.

Lesson Objectives

Recognize that you can identify minerals by their color, luster, hardness, streak, and specific gravity.

PREPARE

Approximate lesson time is 60 minutes.

Advance Preparation

- In this science lesson, your student will be using the rock kit. For the first few lessons in this unit, we don't want her to know the identity of the different rocks and minerals. Remove the lid with the key from the box, and set it aside for later reference.
- A white, porcelain streak plate is included in K12's additional science materials. If you do not have the plate, you will need to purchase at a home improvement store. The plate is a 2 inch piece of white ceramic tile.

Materials

For the Student

Mineral Information List
Mystery Minerals
coin - penny
flashlight
K12 Rocks and Minerals Kit
nail, iron
tile - porcelain streak plate, white
Specific Gravity
bowl - 2 liter
spring scale
string - 60 cm
water

Keywords and Pronunciation

dolomite (DOH-luh-miyt)

galena (guh-LEE-nuh)

Hematite (HEE-muh-tiyt)

luster: The way light reflects off the surface of a mineral, or its shine. A silver coin has a metallic luster.

mica (MIY-kuh)

olivine (AH-luh-veen)

pyrite (PIY-riyt)

spinel (spuh-NEL)

LEARN

Activity 1: Qualities of Minerals *(Online)*

Safety

As always, you may wish to preview any websites before your student views them.

Activity 2: Be a Geologist *(Offline)*

Practice your skills as a geologist as you test mystery minerals and identify them based on their color, luster, hardness, and streak. See how many you can get correct—you may be headed for a career on the rocks!

ASSESS

Lesson Assessment: Properties of Minerals *(Offline)*

Have an adult review your answers to the Mystery Minerals activity and input the results online.

LEARN

Activity 3: Optional: Specific Gravity *(Offline)*

If you think you are ready for the big time in geology, put your minerals through a specific gravity test.

Name _____ Date _____

Properties of Minerals

Mineral Information List

Mineral	Color	Luster	Streak	Hardness	Specific Gravity
Flourite	White, blue, green, red, yellow, purple	Glassy	Colorless	4	3 to 3.2
Feldspar	Gray, white, pink	Glassy	Colorless	6	2.5
Topaz	White, pink, yellow, pale blue	Glassy	Colorless	8	3.5
Pyrite	Gold	Metallic	Black	6	5.2
Quartz	Colorless, milky	Glassy	Colorless	7	2.6
Talc	Grayish, white	Dull	White	1	2.8
Gypsum	Colorless, white	Glassy	White	2	2.3
Hornblende	Dark green	Glassy	Pale gray	5.5	3.2
Calcite	Colorless, white	Glassy	Colorless, white	3	2.7
Halite	Colorless, light pink or red	Glassy	White	2 to 2.5	2.2

Name _____   Date _____

Properties of Minerals

Mystery Minerals

Imagine a conversation like this:

>FRIEND: I found this big hard lump in my backyard—I think I found gold!
>YOU: Are you sure you've found real gold?
>FRIEND: It's gold colored. Of course it's gold! Right?

What would you say to your friend?

Geologists test minerals in many different ways before saying for sure what substances are in them. Those tests include color, as your friend observed. But they also include hardness, luster, streak, and specific gravity. Each mineral has its own properties that make it different from all other minerals.

Test the items in your kit and find out what minerals they contain.

Materials

Nail

K12 Rocks & Minerals Kit

Penny

Flashlight

Streak plate

Magnifying Glass

Procedure

Remove minerals 10, 11, 12, 13, 14, and 15 from your K12 Rocks and Minerals Kit. Perform each of the following tests on each mineral, and record your observations in the table provided.

Test 1: Color

Use the magnifying glass to observe each sample. Describe the color of each sample and write your observations in the chart on page 2.

Test 2: Luster

Hold each sample up to the sunlight or under the flashlight. Observe and record how light reflects off it. Luster may be a metallic shine, a glassy radiance, or a pearly shimmer.

Test 3: Streak

Use each mineral to draw a line across the streak plate. Observe and record the color of each streak.

Test 4: Hardness

Use your fingernail, the copper penny, and the nail to test the hardness of each mineral. Try to scratch each sample with these items. Try to scratch each sample with each of the other minerals. Give each sample a number from Moh's Scale of Hardness that describes its hardness. A number 1 on the scale is the softest, while 10 is the hardest.

Observations

Mineral	10	11	12	13	14	15
Color						
Luster						
Streak						
Hardness						
Mineral name						

Analysis

Use your observations and study the Mineral Information List to figure out the identity of each mineral. Write their names in the last column in the chart.

Conclusion

1. How are the minerals you tested different from each other?

   _____

2. When scientists study things, they organize them into groups, or *classify* them, based on what they have in common. How does classifying make science easier?

   _____

   _____

3. Check your answers for mineral names. Did you have any that were incorrect? What do scientists do when testing to make sure they get their tests right?

   _____

   _____

Name _____   Date _____

Properties of Minerals

Specific Gravity

Density can be used to identify any substance. Minerals have definite chemicals inside them, as well as physical characteristics on the outside. Density can be used to identify minerals based on these characteristics.

Sometimes, two minerals are too close in density to be identified. In that case, scientists measure the minerals' specific gravities. *Specific gravity* is simply a comparison of the mass of a mineral to the volume of water it displaces. Try this investigation to find the specific gravities of rocks from your K12 Rocks & Minerals Kit. Then compare your results to the specific gravities listed in the Mineral Information List.

Materials

2-liter bowl	hematite	water	talc
String, 60 cm	gypsum	feldspar	calcite
hornblende	pyrite	quartz	spring scale

Procedure

1. Fill the bowl about three-fourths with water.

2. Tie string around the mineral and make a loop in the other end.

3. Hook the string to the spring scale and measure the mass of the mineral in grams. Write the mass on the chart in the column "Mass Out of Water"

4. Keeping the mineral hanging on the scale, lower it into the water in the bowl. Do not allow the mineral to rest on the bottom or sides of the bowl. Write the mass on the chart in the column "Mass in Water."

5. Subtract the mineral's Mass in Water from its Mass Out of Water. Write this new number in the "Mass Displaced" column.

6. Divide the mineral's Mass Out of Water by its Mass Displaced. (Mass Out of Water ÷ Mass Displaced.) This is your mineral's specific gravity. Compare your findings to the Mineral Information List.

Mineral	Mass out of water (g)	Mass in water (g)	Mass displaced (g)	Specific gravity (g)
Feldspar				
Hornblende				
Quartz				
Hematite				
Talc				
Gypsum				
Calcite				
Pyrite				

Student Guide

Mining of Minerals

There are over 90 minerals that humans use in different industries. These minerals are found inside the Earth and must be mined. Once mined, people must take these minerals from rocks and process them. In this lesson you will learn about some activities involved in getting the minerals we use.

Lesson Objectives

- Define ore as rock with a high metal content.
- Describe some of the everyday uses of minerals.
- Describe the activity of producing aluminum from bauxite as an example of processing ore.

PREPARE

Approximate lesson time is 60 minutes.

Materials

For the Student

> Minerals All Around
> Minerals Around the World Map
> household item - see Minerals All Around sheet
> pencil

Keywords and Pronunciation

ore: Rock with a high metal content. Bingham Canyon Mine processes a great deal of copper ore.

surface mining: A form of mining that strips off the surface layer of earth and digs down to the mineral-containing layers. Huge explosions at the surface-mining site lifted layers off of the ground for the miners.

talus (TAY-luhs)

LEARN

Activity 1: Metals from the Earth *(Online)*

Safety

As always, you may wish to preview any websites before your student views them.

Activity 2: If It Can't be Grown, It Has to Be Mined *(Offline)*

Forks, spoons, dishwashers and microwave ovens—what do they all have in common? They are made from minerals. But minerals can be found in every room of the house, not just the kitchen. Learn more about how things you use every day are made from minerals.

ASSESS

Lesson Assessment: Mining of Minerals *(Offline)*

You will complete an offline assessment covering the main objectives of this lesson. Your learning coach will score this assessment.

LEARN

Activity 3: Visit the Mineral Information Institute *(Online)*

There is a lot to learn about minerals and mining. Did you know that the mineral *gold* has played an important role throughout history? Visit the Mineral Information Institute to learn about gold and many other minerals.

Go to the next screen to get started.

Safety

As usual, you may wish to preview any books or websites listed in this lesson.

Name _____   Date _____

Mining of Minerals

Minerals All Around

Almost all of the things we use every day are made from minerals. All the items you use at home, at play, to do work, and even some things we eat come from minerals that are mined from the Earth.

Look around your house for the following objects. Observe the objects and predict what minerals might be in them. Then, look them up on the Minerals All Around List. Were you surprised?

Minerals can be found in countries all around the world. Some countries, such as the U.S. and Russia, have many different minerals mined from them. Where do all of the minerals come from that make up the paper this is written on, or the pencil you are using? Use the Where in the World List to record the countries where the minerals can be found.

Common household items	Minerals I predict may be in them	Minerals actually in them	Where they are mined
Drinking glass			
Fruit juice			
Pencil			
Soda can			

How could a friend who doesn't know much about minerals see where they come from? A map! You now have all the information you need to show where in the world these minerals come from. Think of a symbol, such as a triangle or star, for each mineral in your table. Use these symbols to show what countries they are mined in on the world map. Be sure to create a key so that your friend can read your map.

Minerals All Around List

Baby Powder: Talc

Batteries: Antimony, Cadmium, Lead, Zinc

Bicycle: Aluminum, Clay, Diatomite, Mica, Sulfur, Selenium, Wollastonite, Zinc

Books: Clay, Limestone, Sodium Sulfate, Feldspar

Bricks: Bauxite, Chromite, Zircon, Silica, Graphite, Kyanite, Andalusite, Sillimanite, Clays

Cake/Bread: Gypsum, Phosphates

Car: Platinum, Iron, Aluminum, Lead, Coal, Barite, Boron, Calcium Carbonate, Bentonite, Silica, Chromium, Perlite, Wollastonite, Mica, Industrial Diamonds, Zeolite, Clays

Carpet: Calcium Carbonate, Limestone

Clothing: Boron, Halite, Molybdenum, Sulfur

Desk: Copper, Iron, Zinc, Nickel

Digital Alarm Clock: Boron, Copper, Gold, Quartz

Drinking Glass: Boron, Silica

Drinking Water: Limestone, Lime, Salt, Fluorite

Fruit Juice: Perlite, Diatomite

Glass/Ceramics: Silica sand, Limestone, Talc, Lithium, Borates, Soda Ash, Feldspar

Ink: Calcium Carbonate

Lights: Aluminum, Copper, Beryllium (fluorescent), Tungsten (incandescent), Tin, Nickel

Linoleum: Calcium Carbonate, Clay, Wollastonite

Kitty Litter: Attapulgite, Montmorillonite, Zeolites, Diatomite, Pumice, Volcanic Ash

Paint: Titanium Oxide, Clays, Limestone, Mica, Talc, Silica, Copper, Fluorspar, Iron, Tungsten, Zinc, Cadmium

Paper: Boron, Clay, Kaolin, Sulfur, Talc, Titanium, Trona

Pencils: Graphite, Clay

Pencil Sharpener: Iron, Copper, Zinc

Plastic: Limestone, Wollastonite, Coal, Talc, Silica, Petroleum Products

Pots and Pans: Aluminum, Iron, copper

Potting Soil: Titanium Dioxide, Kaolin Clays, Calcium Carbonate, Mica, Talc, Silica, Wollastonite

Skateboard: Aluminum, Calcium Carbonate, Clay, Coal, Iron, Mica, Sulfur, Silica, Talc, Wollastonite

Soda Can: Aluminum

Sports Equipment: Graphite, Fiberglass

Telephone: Aluminum, Beryllium, Coal, Copper, Gold, Iron, Limestone, Silica, Silver, Talc, Wollastonite

Television set: Aluminum, Antimony, Barite, Beryllium, Cobalt, Columbium, Copper, Europium, Gallium, Germanium, Gold, Indium, Iron, Kaolin, Lanthanides, Limestone, Lithium, Manganese, Mercury, Mica, Molybdenum, Platinum, Rhenium, Selenium, Silica, Strontium, Tantalum, Tellurium, Terbium, Tin, Titanium, Vanadium, Yttrium, Zinc, Zirconium

Toothpaste: Calcium Carbonate, Limestone, Sodium Carbonate, Fluorite

Wallpaper: Mica, Trona

Where in the World List

Aluminum (Bauxite): Australia, Guinea

Andalusite: South Africa, India

Barite: China, India

Beryllium: US, Russia

Borates: Turkey, US

Cadmium: Japan, Belgium

Chromite: South Africa, Russia

Clays: US

Copper: Chile, US

Diatomite: US, France, Romania

Feldspar: Italy, US

Fluorspar: China, Mongolia

Graphite: Korea, India

Gravel: US

Gypsum: US, Canada

Industrial Diamonds: Australia, Dem Rep of the Congo

Iron: Russia, China

Kyanite: South Africa, India, France

Lead: Australia, US

Lime: Russia, China

Limestone: US

Micas: US, Russia

Nickel: Russia, Canada

Perlite: US, Greece

Platinum: South Africa, Russia

Potash: Russia, Canada

Pumice: Italy, Greece

Selenium: Japan, Canada

Silica Sand: US, Netherlands

Sillimanite: South Africa

Sodium Sulfate: Mexico, Spain

Sulfur: US, Russia

Talc: Japan, US

Tin: China, Brazil

Titanium: Russia, Japan

Trona (Soda Ash) : US, Kenya

Tungsten: China, Russia

Vermiculite: South Africa, US

Wollastonite: Germany, Great Britain

Zeolites: US, Tanzania

Zinc: Canada, Australia

Zircon: Australia, South Africa

Name _____   Date _____

Mining of Minerals
Minerals Around the World

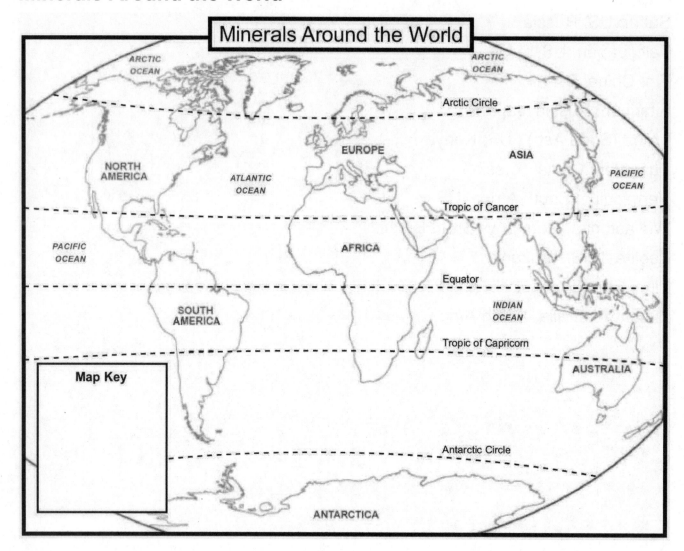

Student Guide
The Rock Cycle

Few things seem more changeless than rocks. So you would think that of all the things in nature, rocks are some of the most stable. Over long periods of time, however, rocks change. In fact, they can change in many ways, recycling their minerals into the same or other kinds of rocks. This fascinating process is called *the rock cycle*.

Lesson Objectives

- Describe what is meant by the term *rock cycle*.
- Identify the three different types of rocks and how they form.

PREPARE

Approximate lesson time is 60 minutes.

Materials

For the Student
  Rock Formation
  K12 Rocks and Minerals Kit
  Rock Recipes
  Pencil
  chocolate chips - 75 g (1/2 cup)
  egg
  flour - 150 g (1 cup + 2 tbls.)
  household item - vanilla (1/2 tsp.)
  measuring spoon
  sugar - 125 g (2/3 cup)
  bowl - large mixing
  butter - 75 g (2 1/2 tbls.)
  cookie sheet - greased
  measuring cup
  spoon

Keywords and Pronunciation

gneiss (niys)

igneous (IG-nee-uhs): A class of rocks that forms from magma and lava. Obsidian may look like black glass but, in fact, it is a kind of igneous rock.

metamorphic (meh-tuh-MOR-fik): A class of rocks that forms when heat and pressure act on igneous or sedimentary rock.

metamorphosis (meh-tuh-MOR-fuh-suhs): the process of change in the shape or composition of rocks, caused by heat, pressure, or chemical reactions acting over time

rock cycle: The pathways by which rocks change from one form to another over time. Igneous rocks and metamorphic rocks are part of the rock cycle.

sediment: Layers of rock and mud that form at the bottom of lakes, streams, rivers, and oceans. The sediment at the bottom of the bay is mostly mud.

sedimentary: Rocks that form when other rocks layer and fuse with each other. Sandstone is a kind of sedimentary rock.

LEARN

Activity 1: Ever-Changing Rocks (Online)

Activity 2: Rock Formation (Offline)

What do sandstone, gneiss, and pumice have in common? They are all examples of one of the main types of rock—sedimentary, metamorphic, and igneous. Take a closer look at these rocks and review where they form.

Activity 3: Rock Recipes (Online)

Have you ever helped cook a meal in which you had to follow a recipe? What were the ingredients like? In this activity you will be asked to write some recipes of your own, but they are not for things you can eat—they are recipes for rocks!

Safety

As always, you may wish to preview any websites before your student views them.

ASSESS

Lesson Assessment: The Rock Cycle (Offline)

You will complete an offline assessment covering the main objectives of this lesson. Your learning coach will score this assessment.

LEARN

Activity 4: Optional: Metamorphic Rock Cookies *(Offline)*

What do chocolate chip cookies and metaphoric rocks have in common? The ingredients for chocolate chip cookes are something like the minerals in metamorphic rock. When you heat the mixture, it changes into something else—in this case, a yummy treat!

Activity Instructions:

125 g (2/3 cup) sugar

1 egg

75 g (1/2 cup) chocolate chips

150 g (1 cup + 2 Tbls) flour

75 g (2 ½ Tbls) butter, softened

½ teaspoon vanilla

1. Preheat the oven to 375 degrees.
2. Cream the butter and sugar together until the mixture is light and fluffy.
3. Beat in the egg and add the vanilla.
4. Slowly add the flour.
5. Stir in the chocolate chips.
6. Drop spoonfuls of cookie dough onto a greased cookie sheet, leaving 3 cm between each cookie.
7. Bake the cookies for 10-15 minutes or until they are golden brown. While they cool, explain how the chocolate chip cookies are like metamorphic rocks. When they are cool, enjoy your metamorphic treat!

Safety

This lesson involves eating or working with food. Before beginning, check with your doctor, if necessary, to find out whether your student will have any allergic reaction to the food.

Name _____   Date _____

The Rock Cycle
Rock Formation

Many of the samples in your rock kit are examples of sedimentary, metamorphic or igneous rock. Take the pumice, basalt, limestone, sandstone, marble and gneiss samples out of the kit.

Match the word in the Word Bank to its correct description.

Word Bank

igneous rock   gneiss

pumice   sedimentary rock

basalt   limestone

metamorphic rock   sandstone

marble

1. _____ A class of rocks formed when heat and pressure act on igneous or sedimentary rock. Marble, which is an example of this kind of rock, forms under great pressure.

2. _____ This metamorphic rock is dark but looks like it has stripes of minerals running through it. The visible crystals make it shimmer.

3. _____ This rock is formed by cooled lava filled with gas bubbles. It is white or light gray and might look like a rock froth.

4. _____ Layers may be visible in this reddish-brown sedimentary rock.

5. _____ Rocks that form when other rocks are cemented together. Sandstone is an example of this kind of rock.

6. _____ This metamorphic rock is white and sparkles with crystals that are easy to see.

7. _____ A class of rocks formed from magma and lava.

8. _____ This rock is volcanic rock, so it is igneous. It is dark gray and very hard. You may see holes in it made by gas bubbles.

9. _____ This whitish-gray sedimentary rock is powdery, with few visible crystals.

Study the picture. Use the words from the Word Bank to correctly label the picture.

Word Bank

igneous rock   metamorphic rock   sedimentary rock

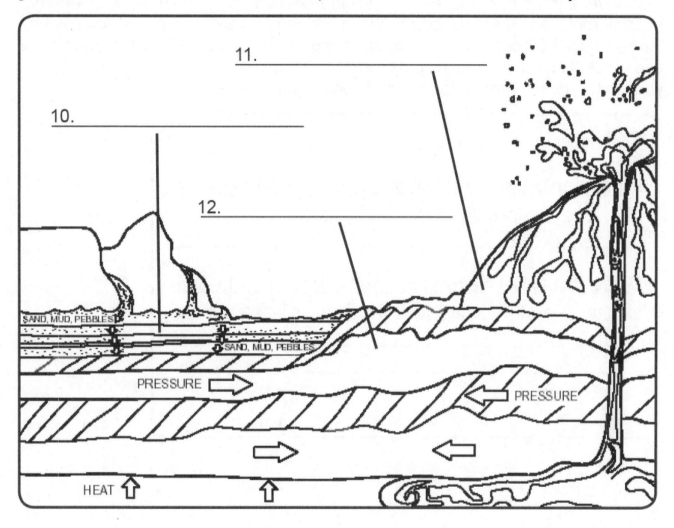

Name _____   Date _____

The Rock Cycle

Rock Recipes

You have learned how it takes several different factors to make up sedimentary, metamorphic, and igneous rocks, such as minerals, heat, and pressure. You can think of each of these components as an ingredient that goes into the "recipe" for each rock. Look at the example recipe card for igneous rocks, and then write your own recipe for metamorphic and sedimentary rocks.

Title <u>Igneous Rock Recipe</u> _____

Ingredients <u>1 part metamorphic or sedimentary rock</u> _____
                <u>25 parts heat</u> _____

_____

Directions <u>Heat the rocks to 1,400°C for 6 hours to form</u>
<u>magma. Allow the magma to cool to form an igneous rock.</u>

_____

_____

Title _____

Ingredients _____

_____

_____

Directions _____

_____

_____

_____

Title _____

Ingredients _____

_____

_____

Directions _____

_____

_____

_____

Student Guide
Drifting Continents

The great movements of the earth happen both on and below its surface. Magma from the mantle is constantly moving, exerting a powerful force on the crust above. Huge plates on the surface rearrange themselves like moving puzzle pieces. Take a look at how this *continental drift* has occurred throughout the earth's long history.

Lesson Objectives

- Describe Alfred Wegener's theory of continental drift.
- Describe three types of plate boundaries.
- Explain that earth's crust is made up of rigid plates that are always moving.

PREPARE

Approximate lesson time is 60 minutes.

Materials

For the Student

> Pangaea Puzzle
> paper, construction, 9" x 12"
> scissors
> Plate Boundaries
> pencil
> Mountain Model
> clay
> hairpins
> household item - roll of calculator paper
> cardboard - sheet 12 x 20 inches
> ruler, metric
> tape, masking
> tissue paper - two or three colors

Keywords and Pronunciation

Alfred Wegener (AHL-frayt VAY-guh-nuhr)

Himalaya (hih-muh-LAY-uh)

oceanic (oh-shee-A-nihk)

Pangaea (pan-JEE-uh): the name scientists give to a supercontinent that once existed on earth

San Andreas (san an-DRAY-uhs)

Theory of Plate Tectonics: the scientific theory that earth's crust is made up of about 20 huge plates that are always moving very slowly

LEARN

Activity 1: Pangaea Puzzle *(Offline)*

Can you name the seven continents? Scientists think that long ago, all seven continents were a part of one huge continent, which they name *Pangaea*. Before you learn more about why scientists think the continents have drifted apart, put together your Pangaea Puzzle.

Activity 2: Movement of Continents *(Online)*

Activity 3: Plate Boundaries *(Offline)*

Amazing things can happen when the edges of plates move. Review what happens when plates push against each other or slide past each other.

ASSESS

Lesson Assessment: Drifting Continents *(Offline)*

You will complete an offline assessment covering the main objectives of this lesson. Your learning coach will score this assessment.

LEARN

Activity 4: Optional: Mountain Models *(Offline)*

Have you ever seen a mountain form itself? Of course not—it takes a long, long time. Complete the activity on the Mountain Model sheet to see what happens when two continental plates collide with each other.

Name _____   Date _____

Drifting Continents
Pangaea Puzzle

Cut out the pieces from the world map and place them on a piece of construction paper. Move the pieces around to see how they might have fit together to form Pangaea. You will see how they come together in the Explore section.

Name _____ Date _____

Drifting Continents

Plate Boundaries

Look at the pictures of the different plates moving against each other. Describe what is happening in each picture and what the results may be.

Description:

_____

_____

Results:

_____

_____

_____

Description:

_____

_____

Results:

_____

_____

_____

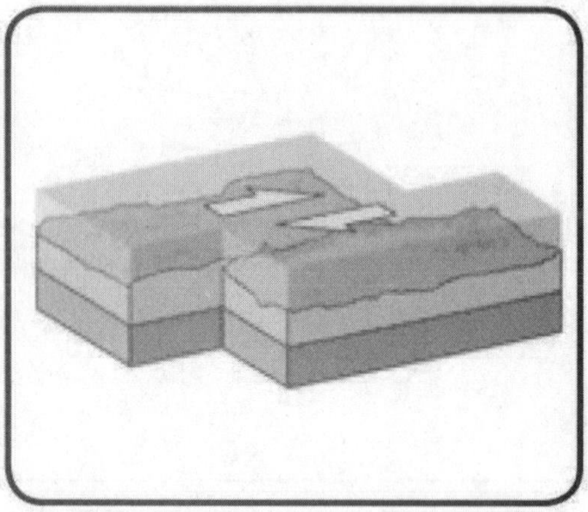

Description:

_____

_____

Results:

_____

_____

_____

Name _____ Date _____

Drifting Continents

Mountain Model

Complete the following steps to make your Mountain Model. Use the illustration to help you.

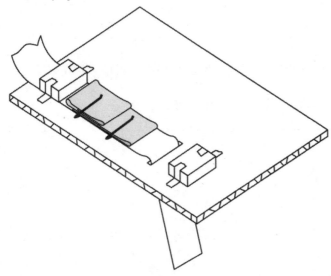

1. In a 50 cm by 30 cm piece of cardboard, cut a slit that is 10 cm long.

2. Cut a piece of calculator paper so that it is at least 75 cm long.

3. Form pieces of clay into two blocks that are the same width of the paper and about 5 cm high. These will represent the two plates.

4. Thread one end of the calculator paper through the slit so that you can pull it from the bottom of the cardboard.

5. Use masking tape to secure one of the clay blocks at the end of the cardboard about 1 cm behind the slit. Tape the other block on the end of the paper that is on top of the cardboard.

6. Cut tissue paper into strips as wide as the paper. Use hairpins to attach four layers of tissue paper directly in front of the clay block at the end of the paper.

7. Slowly pull on the paper coming out of the bottom of the cardboard so that the clay block at the end moves toward the slit.

8. Continue to pull on the paper until it can't move anymore and observe what happens.

   What happened to the tissue paper when the two blocks collided?

   _____

   _____

Student Guide

Volcanoes

Volcanoes are among the most awesome things on the Earth's surface. Often they explode with tremendous force. They can cause great destruction, as well as fiery displays of light and noise. Find out what volcanoes are and what causes them, and learn about the different types.

Lesson Objectives

- Explain how volcanoes are formed.
- Identify and describe the three types of land volcanoes (cinder cone, composite, and shield).
- Identify the main parts of a volcano: magma chamber, vent, and crater.

PREPARE

Approximate lesson time is 60 minutes.

Materials

For the Student

> Volcanoes
> pencil

Keywords and Pronunciation

lava: magma that is extruded to the surface of the Earth's crust

magma: Molten rock that is under the surface of the earth. The upper crust and lower mantle are places where magma is found.

Paricutin (pahr-REE-koo-teen)

volcano: Any areas of the Earth in which magma is extruded to the surface. Most volcanoes are situated at the edges of continental plates.

LEARN

Activity 1: The Fire from Below (Online)

Safety

As usual, you may wish to preview any books or websites listed in this lesson.

Activity 2: Volcanoes (Offline)

You have learned a lot about the different types of volcanoes. Review these volcanoes and the parts that make up each of them.

ASSESS

Lesson Assessment: Volcanoes *(Online)*

You will complete an online assessment covering the main objectives of this lesson. Your assessment will be scored by the computer.

LEARN

Activity 3: Optional: Volcanoes Around the World *(Offline)*

Visit Volcano World to discover volcanoes in countries all around the world.

Safety

As always, you may wish to preview any websites before your student views them.

Name _____   Date _____

Volcanoes

You have learned about three types of land volcanoes: cinder cone, shield and composite. Label each of these volcanoes. Then, on the lines below each volcano, write a description of each and how it formed. If needed, look back at the Explore section to help you.

_____

_____

_____

_____

_____

_____

_____

_____

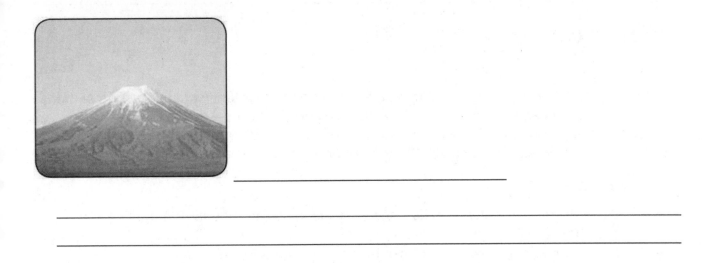

_____

_____

_____

_____

_____

Label the magma chamber, vent and crater on the picture of the volcano below.

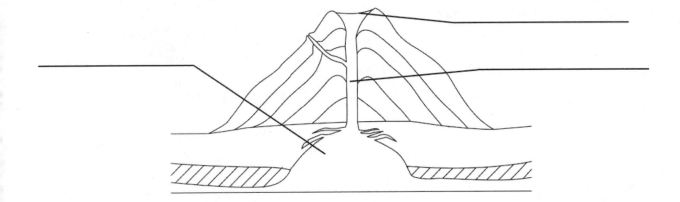

Student Guide

Earthquakes

Lots of things change in life, but you'd think the Earth under your feet wouldn't be one of them. One experience with an earthquake, though, can change your *mind*—and fast. Earthquakes are fascinating and frightening events of nature. Why do they happen? Can we predict when they will strike? How is the Earth itself changed after a massive quake?

Lesson Objectives

- Describe how the *Richter scale* is used to measure an earthquake's magnitude.
- Explain how a *seismograph* is used to determine earthquake activity.
- State that an *earthquake* is the shaking or sliding of the Earth's surface.

PREPARE

Approximate lesson time is 60 minutes.

Materials

For the Student

>Model Seismograph
>cardboard box - 30 cm (12 in) each side
>hole punch - (single punch)
>household item - Paper cup, 5 oz. (2)
>marbles
>marker, black water soluble
>paper, adding machine tape
>pencil
>ruler, metric
>scissors
>string
>tape, masking
>Earthquake!
>household item - glue
>household item - paper
>thumbtacks
>wood block - 2 of same size

Keywords and Pronunciation

epicenter: The point on the Earth's surface that is right above the focus of an earthquake. The greatest damage was done at the epicenter of the quake.

fault: A break in the Earth's crust along which plates move. The San Andreas Fault in California is the site of many earthquakes.

focus: The point where the movement of the plates started. The earthquake that caused so much damage had a focus deep within the Earth.

Richter (RIHK-tuhr)

seismograph (SIYZ-muh-graf): An instrument used to record earthquake waves. The seismograph recorded a large earthquake at 10:05 a.m.

seismologist (siyz-MAH-luh-jist)

tsunami (tsou-NAH-mee)

LEARN

Activity 1: The Big Shake *(Online)*

Safety

As usual, you may wish to preview any books or websites listed in this lesson.

Activity 2: Model Seismograph *(Offline)*

Scientists use seismographs to measure earthquake activity. The lines drawn on the paper help the scientists determine the magnitude of the earthquake on the Richter scale. Make your own seismograph, and then brace yourself for the quakes!

ASSESS

Lesson Assessment: Earthquakes *(Online)*

You will complete an online assessment covering the main objectives of this lesson. Your assessment will be scored by the computer.

LEARN

Activity 3: Optional: Earthquake! *(Offline)*

Make a model of an earthquake using two wooden blocks, a piece of paper, and some thumbtacks. Watch what happens when the "earth" shakes during the great quake.

Safety

Caution your student to be careful when working with the thumbtacks in the Beyond the Lesson activity.

Name _____   Date _____

Earthquakes

Model Seismograph

Follow the steps below to make your own seismograph.

1. Turn the box on its side so that the opening is facing you. Cut the flaps off of each side of the box so that the opening is not blocked.

2. Cut a circle with a 4 cm (2 in.) diameter in the center of the top of the box.

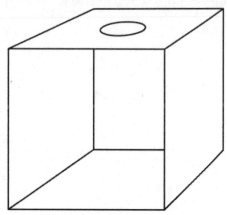

3. Cut two slits in the box. The slits should be 1 cm x 8 cm (1/2 in x 4 in.). The first slit should be made in the center of the bottom of the box, close to the edge. The second slit should be lined up with the first one, but made at the back of the box.

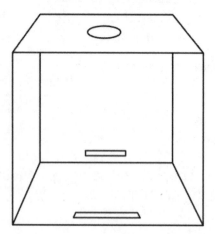

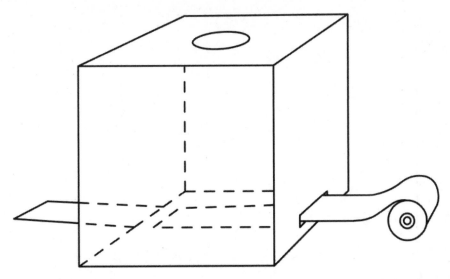

4. Place the roll of adding tape at the back of the box so that the end of the paper comes over the top of the roll. Thread the paper through the slit at the back of the box and then down into the slit at the front.

5. Use a hole punch to make two holes below the rim of the cup, one on each side. Then use a pencil to poke a hole in the center of the bottom of the cup.

6. Thread a 60 cm (24 in.) piece of string through the two holes in the sides of the cup.

7. Lay a pencil across the hole in the top of the box and tape the two ends of the string to it.

8. Push the tip of a marker through the bottom of the cup. Add some small rocks or marbles to the cup to act as weights.

9. Turn the pencil at the top of the box until the tip of the pen barely touches the paper beneath it, then tape the string to secure it at this length to the pencil. Tape the ends of the pencil to the top of the box.

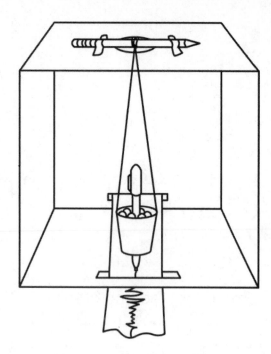

10. Pull the end of the paper forward with one hand as you gently shake the box with your other hand. The shaking will simulate an earthquake.

11. Repeat step 10 to simulate a second earthquake, this time shaking the box a little bit harder.

The pen in the cup made markings on the paper as you pulled it. What happened to the markings as you shook the box to simulate an earthquake?

_____

_____

How can you tell by looking at the paper which earthquake was stronger?

_____

_____

What is the name of the scale that scientists use to determine the magnitude of an earthquake?

_____

_____

Name _____   Date _____

Earthquakes

Earthquake!

You have learned that earthquakes occur when two continental plates slide against each other moving in opposite directions. Build a model of an earthquake to explore what happens as the ground shakes.

Directions

1. Place the two wooden blocks side-by-side lengthwise. Glue a piece of paper on top of the blocks. Be careful not to get glue in between the blocks or they will not slide against each other.

2. Carefully lay some thumbtacks on top of the paper with the pointed sides up.

3. Push the ends of the blocks in opposite directions. Observe what happens.

Questions

1. What do the two wooden blocks represent?

   _____

2. What happened when you pushed the two blocks in opposite directions?

   _____

   _____

   _____

3. How does this activity show what happens during an earthquake?

   _____

   _____

   _____

Student Guide

Rocks and Minerals: Unit Review and Assessment

The United States Geological Survey (USGS), is a government agency that collects, monitors, and analyzes information about natural resources in the United States and around the world. They have an information center people can call to ask questions about rocks, minerals, volcanoes, earthquakes—anything about the Earth. Today, you have been asked to volunteer at the information center and answer some calls. Don't worry—if you need help, you can ask your boss, Paula.

Lesson Objectives

- Describe what happens during an earthquake and how the landscape can change as a result.
- Differentiate among igneous, sedimentary, and metamorphic rocks by referring to their properties and methods of formation.
- Explain that rock is composed of different combinations of minerals.
- Explain that the surface of the Earth is made up of rigid plates that are in constant motion, and that the motion of these plates against, over, and under each other causes earthquakes, volcanoes, and the formation of mountains.
- Identify and describe the properties of the Earth's layers: crust, mantle, outer core, and inner core.
- Identify the various structures of volcanoes, describe the types of eruptions that form them, and explain how they change the landscape.
- Recognize that minerals have their own distinct crystal shape, determined by the arrangement of their atoms.
- Recognize that ore is rock with a high metal content, and that most metals come from minerals mined from the Earth's crust.
- Recognize that you can identify minerals by their color, luster, hardness, streak, and specific gravity.
- Describe how the *Richter scale* is used to measure an earthquake's magnitude.
- Explain how a *seismograph* is used to determine earthquake activity.

PREPARE

Approximate lesson time is 60 minutes.

LEARN

Activity 1: On Call! *(Online)*

ASSESS

Unit Assessment: Rocks and Minerals *(Offline)*

Complete an offline Unit Assessment. Your learning coach will score the assessment.

Student Guide

Weathering

Rocks and minerals are formed and broken down in the turbulent processes of Earth. Rocks formed in huge eruptions of lava may slowly fade away under forces of weathering—wind, water, and even the workings of living things. These bits of rocks and minerals may form huge sediments. So the Earth, which seems so unchanging is, in fact, always changing.

You have learned that the rock cycle is a continuous process that changes the forms of rocks over time. One of the main steps in the rock cycle is *weathering*, the breakdown of rocks. Learn how rocks get broken apart by nature's forces.

Lesson Objectives

- Describe different causes of weathering, such as ice, growth from plants, and acid rain.
- Identify examples of physical and chemical weathering.

PREPARE

Approximate lesson time is 60 minutes.

Materials

For the Student

Physical and Chemical Weathering
clay
cup, plastic (3)
freezing source
vinegar
chalk
markers
plastic wrap
spoon (2)
water

Keywords and Pronunciation

deposition: The dumping of soil or rock particles in a place far from their origins. The glacier caused the deposition of a huge amount of weathered rock at the mouth of the river.

erosion: The movement of soil and broken rocks by wind, water, or other means. During the Dust Bowl era, wind caused great erosion of the soil.

lichen (LIY-kuhn)

mass wasting: The movement down a slope of a body of rock and/or soil due directly to gravity. Mass wasting can be rapid, as when a landslide or mudflow occurs, or it can be slower, as in a slow creep of a hillside downhill.

sediment: The layers of rock or soil that result from their transport and deposition. The sediment at the bottom of the lake originated as soil on the nearby hills.

weathering: the breakdown of rocks by physical or chemical processes; weathering causes the rocks on a cliff to wear away

LEARN

Activity 1: The Breakdown of Rocks *(Online)*

Activity 2: Physical and Chemical Weathering *(Offline)*

In this activity you will experiment with physical and chemical weathering. These processes break down rocks on the surface of the Earth. Both contribute to the ultimate erosion of rocks.

ASSESS

Lesson Assessment: Weathering *(Online)*

You will complete an online assessment covering the main objectives of this lesson. Your assessment will be scored by the computer.

Name _____   Date _____

Weathering

Physical and Chemical Weathering

Activity 1

1. Moisten two clumps of clay and roll them into two balls.

2. Wrap each ball with plastic wrap. Place one ball in the freezer, and leave one out on the counter for 24 hours.

3. After 24 hours, unwrap the two balls and compare them.

Do the two clay balls still look the same? If not, explain how they look different.

_____

_____

_____

_____

Is this an example of chemical or physical weathering?

_____

_____

_____

Activity 2

1. Break the piece of chalk into three pieces. Place one piece in each of the three cups.

2. Using a marker, write the word *water* on the first cup and *vinegar* on the second.

3. Observe what happens as you pour enough water into the first cup to cover the chalk. Record your answer in the table below. Do the same to the piece in the second cup, this time using vinegar.

4. Place the remaining piece of chalk in the third cup.

5. Set the experiment aside for a couple of days, or until the vinegar and water have evaporated. Compare the chalk in the first two cups to the chalk in the third cup. Record your observations in the table on the next page.

Observations	Immediately after adding the liquid	After the liquid has evaporated
Chalk in water		
Chalk in vinegar		

Is what happened to the chalk an example of chemical or physical weathering?

_____

_____

_____

What in nature is causing weathering like the vinegar?

_____

_____

_____

Student Guide
Soils

You have been studying a lot about minerals and rocks lately. There is another element to geology as well—soil. You might think of it as just the dirt beneath your feet. But soil is the very stuff of our lives. Soils are what plants grow in, and plants are the beginning of any food chain. Soils differ widely from place to place and have a lot to them. They are a far cry from "just dirt."

Lesson Objectives

- Describe a soil profile and explain how different horizons are formed.
- Describe properties of various soil types.

PREPARE

Approximate lesson time is 60 minutes.

Advance Preparation

- For this science lesson, you will need three 2-liter plastic bottles.

Materials

For the Student

What's in Your Soil?
household item - craft stick
household item - newspaper
household item - shovel
bottle, plastic - (2 liter) (3)
magnifying glass
markers - permanent
plastic wrap
ruler, metric
scissors
soil - samples

Keywords and Pronunciation

fertile: Capable of supporting plant growth. The gardener said that the lush growth of petunias was due to the fertile soil.

horizon: One of the layers in a soil profile. The A horizon of my soil sample was loaded with earthworms and ants.

humus (HYOO-muhs): Organic matter in the soil, which is the remains of decayed and decaying living things. The farmer was happy with the new land because the soil was rich in humus.

LEARN

Activity 1: Amazing Soil *(Online)*

Activity 2: What's in Your Soil? *(Offline)*

There are many different types of soil containing rocks, particles and organic matter. Explore some soil samples from where you live to see what they are made up of.

Safety

Be careful where you help your student dig up the soil. Check with your local utility company to find out where electrical lines may be buried.

ASSESS

Lesson Assessment: Soils *(Offline)*

You will complete an offline assessment covering the main objectives of this lesson. Your learning coach will score this assessment.

Name _____ Date _____

Soils

What's In Your Soil?

You have learned that soil is a mixture of weathered rock, humus, air, and water. Soils from different areas can be made up of different amounts of these materials. Compare three different soil samples to see what they are made of. Go to different areas to collect them. As you gather your samples, you should be digging down deep enough to be able to observe some horizon layers.

1. Cut the tops off of three 2-liter plastic bottles. These will be used to hold your soil samples.

2. Gather your samples by going to three different locations. Using your shovel, outline a circle and try to dig straight down. For each sample, dig about 20 cm (8 in.) below the surface. Push the top of the empty bottle down through the dirt, carefully lifting it out with the sample inside.

3. Use a permanent marker to label the bottles, noting where each sample was taken from.

4. Look at each sample through the bottle to see if you can clearly observe different layers in the soil. Think about what you have learned about the horizons in a soil profile. Record which horizon(s) your sample contains in the Soil Chart on the next page.

5. Spread three sheets of newspaper out on a large, flat surface. Gently take each sample out of the bottles and place them onto separate pieces of newspaper. Be careful not to mix the samples.

6. Use a magnifying glass to study the contents of each sample. A craft stick can be used to spread the soil around so that things can be seen more clearly. Look for any animals, rocks, plants or decaying material. What type of parent soil do you think this is? Remember, sandy soils have large mineral particles. Clay has small particles. Silts have medium-sized particles. Record your observations in the chart on the next page.

7. Carefully fold the sides of the newspaper up, and pour each sample back into its bottle.

8. Add enough water to each bottle so that it stands at least 4 cm above the soil. Use a different spoon to stir up each sample for about a minute. Allow the samples to sit for a day. Sketch the sample and then describe it in the columns on the next page.

Sample	Location	Soil horizons	Contents	Watered sample sketch	Watered sample description
Sample 1					
Sample 2					
Sample 3					

Student Guide
Erosion and Deposition: Gravity and Water

Soil forms from broken rocks and minerals, humus, air, and water. Soil, too, is a part of the great recycling of materials on Earth. It can be uprooted from its place of origin and moved away by the forces of gravity and water. Erosion and mass wasting remove soil and other materials from the land.

Lesson Objectives

- Describe how gravity and moving water weather, erode, and shape the surface of the land by transporting sediment from one location to another, where it is deposited.
- Describe how the slope of the land affects erosion.
- Generate or compare multiple solutions to reduce the impacts of natural Earth processes on humans.
- Generate or compare multiple solutions to reduce the impacts of natural Earth processes on Michigan's people and places.

PREPARE

Approximate lesson time is 60 minutes.

Materials

For the Student

Water Erosion
clay - modeling
cup, plastic - 8 oz.
drinking glass
drinking straw
household item - 3 books
cookie sheet
measuring cup
paper towels
pencil
soil
water
How Does Erosion Affect My World? Assignmnet

Keywords and Pronunciation

deposition: The settling of rock and soil after it has been transported by forces causing erosion. The river was blocked by the deposition of soil after the mudslide.

erosion: The movement of soil and rock by agents such as gravity, water, glaciers, and wind. The Badlands of South Dakota show evidence of erosion by wind.

mass wasting: The movement down a slope of a body of rock and/or soil due directly to gravity. Mass wasting can be rapid, as when a landslide or mudflow occurs, or it can be slower, as in a slow creep of a hillside downhill.

tributary: A smaller river or creek that carries water into a larger river. The Ohio River is a tributary of the Mississippi River.

V-shaped valley: A valley shaped like a V in cross section, the shape of which is caused by water. Many valleys in California are V-shaped valleys, formed by rushing water.

LEARN

Activity 1: Powers of Gravity and Water *(Online)*

Activity 2: Water Erosion *(Offline)*

Does the slope of the land affect the amount of erosion by water? Complete this activity to see for yourself.

Activity 3: How Does Erosion Affect My World? *(Online and Offline)*

Instructions

You will navigate through this activity and complete the assignment. In the How Does Erosion Affect My World assignment you will be asked to identify local erosion, brainstorm ways to address it and analyze each solution based on merit.

ASSESS

Lesson Assessment: Erosion and Deposition: Gravity and Water *(Online)*

You will complete an online assessment covering the main objectives of this lesson. Your assessment will be scored by the computer.

Name _____   Date _____

Erosion and Deposition: Gravity and Water
Water Erosion

The surface of the Earth is covered with different types of landforms, from small hills to huge, towering mountains. Even though they are different in height, rainfall and gravity working together can cause erosion in all of them.

In this activity, you will run a test to see how the slope of the land affects the amount of water erosion that can occur. A cookie sheet covered in soil will act as the land. A cup filled with water will act as the rainfall. You will run three trials in this experiment, first with one book under one end of the cookie sheet, then with two books, and then finally with three books. The books under the cookie sheet with create a slope in the land like that of a hill or mountain. After you make your prediction, take your supplies outside and perform the activity.

Prediction

Do you think that there will be more water erosion when the "land" is sloped with one, two, or three books?

_____

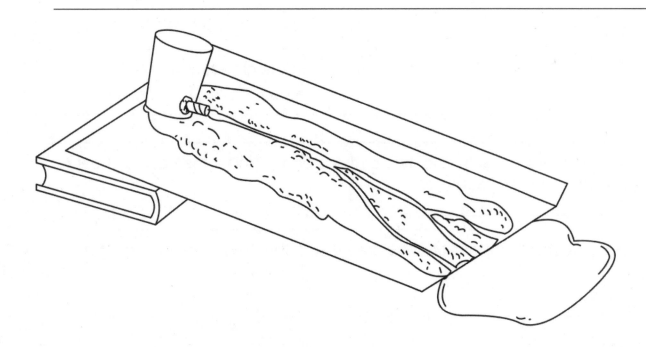

Procedure

1. Fill a drinking glass with water and set it aside.

2. Use a pencil to make a hole in the side of a paper cup. The hole should be down near the bottom of the cup.

3. Cut a straw in half and insert one of the halves into the hole in the cup. Hold the straw in place by sealing it to the cup with bits of clay.

4. Lay a cookie sheet on a flat surface and use a measuring cup to cover it with a thin layer of soil. Place a book under one end of the cookie sheet.

5. Place the cup on the raised end of the cookie sheet.

6. Cover the hole of the straw with your finger as you fill the cup with water.

7. Remove your finger and observe what happens.

8. Use a paper towel to remove the soil and dry off the cookie sheet between each trial. Repeat steps 4 through 7 with two books and then three books under the cookie sheet. Be sure to use the same amount of soil each time.

What happened when you took your finger off the end of the straw and let the water come out?

_____

_____

What two things caused the erosion to happen in the experiment?

_____

_____

Did more erosion occur with one, two or three books under the cookie sheet? Was your prediction correct?

_____

How does this show whether or not slope affects the amount of erosion that occurs?

_____

_____

Name _____   Date _____

Assignment

How Does Erosion Affect My World?

This activity requires you to observe your local landscape to identify areas of erosion. If you are unable to observe your landscape, use your computer to search for local erosion issues.

Procedure:

1. Find an area around your house, public park, or stream that shows evidence of erosion. Describe the area and list the possible causes of erosion.

    Describe the erosion:

    _____

    _____

    Possible causes:

    _____

    _____

2. Brainstorm at least three ideas that could reduce the erosion problem that you observed.

    _____

    _____

    _____

    _____

3. Analyze each solution. List the solution that will work best.

    _____

    _____

Share your answers with your learning coach.

Student Guide

Erosion, Transport, and Deposition: Glaciers and Wind

We have seen that gravity and water are two forces that cause the erosion of rocks and soil. Two others are glaciers and wind. Although glaciers may not seem to affect most of us, they have caused huge changes in the land where many live. Wind is more easily noticed. It is easy to see how wind can pick up soil particles and carry them far away.

Lesson Objectives

- Describe how glaciers are formed and differentiate between the continental and valley glaciers.
- Describe how wind erodes and weathers the surface of the land.
- Explain how glaciers move to erode and reshape the surface of the land.

PREPARE

Approximate lesson time is 60 minutes.

Advance Preparation

- You will need to prepare an ice block ahead of time for this science lesson. Place a cup of water with bits of sand, gravel, and clay into a plastic container and place in the freezer overnight.

Materials

For the Student

Glaciers
cardboard box - top, large with sides
clay
freezing source
household item - additional lamp
household item - plastic container
household item - plastic container top
sand
gravel
lamp
ruler
soil
water

Keywords and Pronunciation

glacier (GLAY-shur): A mass of ice that arises from years of snow adding up. The glacier ended at the ocean where huge chunks of ice fell into the sea.

moraine (muh-RAYN): The mass of earth and ice pushed to the front or side of a moving glacier. Most of the high ports in northern Long Island in New York State are parts of an old moraine.

U-shaped valley: A valley that is rounded at the bottom; formed and given its characteristic shape by a glacier that once inhabited it. There are many U-shaped valleys in Alaska.

LEARN

Activity 1: The Power of Ice and Wind (Online)

Activity 2: Glacial Erosion (Offline)

As glaciers erode the land, they change it a great deal. In this activity, you will make a glacier of your own and see how this erosion occurs.

ASSESS

Lesson Assessment: Erosion, Transport, and Deposition: Glaciers and Wind (Online)

You will complete an online assessment covering the main objectives of this lesson. Your assessment will be scored by the computer.

Name _____ Date _____

Erosion, Transport, and Deposition: Glaciers and Wind

Glaciers

Glaciers are big blocks of ice that may contain bits of rock and soil. For this activity, you will need to make an ice block and allow it to freeze before you can begin. If you have not already done so, fill a plastic container with one cup of water and add bits of sand, clay, and gravel. Place the container in the freezer and allow it to freeze overnight.

Procedure

1. Fill the top of a cardboard box with soil so that it is at least 8 cm (6 in.) deep.

2. Use a ruler to make a V-shaped river valley down the middle of the soil. Measure the channel's width and depth and record them on the table below.

3. Draw a sketch of the river channel in the box below. Be sure to include the measurements.

4. Take your glacier (ice block) out of the freezer and place it at the upper end of the river channel.

5. Using your fingers, gently push the glacier along the river channel until it is in the center of the box top.

6. Place a lamp over the middle of the box top and turn it on. Allow the ice to melt. Observe what happens and record it in the table.

7. Measure the depth and width of the valley created by the glacier.

8. Draw a sketch of the glacier valley including the measurements. Label the moraines and kettle lakes that may have formed.

Valley	Width	Depth	Observation
River Valley			
Glacier Valley			

River Valley Sketch:

Glacier Valley Sketch:

The river valley that you formed in the soil was V-shaped. Describe the shape of the valley that was carved out by the moving glacier.

_____

_____

How can you tell how far down the glacier traveled?

_____

_____

Student Guide
Weathering, Erosion, and Deposition: Unit Review and Assessment

Wow! You have learned a lot about how land can be changed by weathering, erosion, and deposition. Help solve a mystery as you review for your Unit Assessment.

In this lesson you'll meet Mrs. Fussbudget. She is unhappy about a piece of land that she inherited. She thinks that someone has changed it. She doesn't seem to know much about what shapes the land, and how long it takes. Can you help her solve the mystery?

Lesson Objectives

- Describe a soil profile and explain how different horizons are formed.
- Describe how gravity, moving water, wind, and glaciers weather, erode, and shape the surface of the land by transporting sediment from one location to another, where it is deposited.
- Explain both the physical and the chemical weathering of rocks, and be able to classify examples of each.
- Explain that *soil* is a mixture of weathered rock, humus, air, and water.

PREPARE

Approximate lesson time is 60 minutes.

LEARN

Activity 1: Weathering Mystery *(Online)*

ASSESS

Unit Assessment: Weather, Erosion, and Deposition *(Offline)*

Complete an offline Unit Assessment. Your learning coach will score the assessment.

Student Guide

Fossils and How They Form

Dinosaurs, trilobites, and many other once-living things left clues in fossils deep within layers of rock. Find out how fossils formed and meet some important paleontologists who use fossils as clues to the past.

How do we know what the organisms of the past looked like? Fossils are one clue that help scientists called *paleontologists* learn about the past. Come explore the world of fossils, and learn how fossils formed.

Lesson Objectives

- Explain that fossils provide information about organisms that lived long ago.
- Identify the conditions under which fossils may form.
- State that a *fossil* is a trace, print, or remain of an organism preserved over time in a rock.

PREPARE

Approximate lesson time is 60 minutes.

Advance Preparation

- You will need the book *The Fossil Record and the History of Life*, by Bridget Anderson, for all of the lessons in this unit. If you have not yet received this book, skip to the next unit and return to this one later.
- If you don't already have it, you will need dried black beans (1/2 cup), dried red beans (1/2 cup), and dried white beans (1/2 cup) for the Layering activity.

Materials

For the Student

Come Learn with Me: The Fossil Record and the History of Life by Bridget Anderson
Layering
baking dish, rectangular - glass
food - 1/2 cup dried black beans
food - 1/2 cup dried red beans
food - 1/2 cup dried white beans
sand - 1 1/2 cups
bowl (3)
graduated cylinder
measuring cup
spoon
timer

Keywords and Pronunciation

dinosaur: Any animal belonging to a group of large reptiles that lived during the Mesozoic era. Triceratops was the largest horned dinosaur that walked the Earth.

fossil (FAH-suhl)**:** The trace, print, or remain of an organism preserved over time in rock. Fossils can tell us how dinosaurs looked as well as how they acted.

mammoth: A kind of ancient elephant with long, curving tusks and shaggy hair. Mammoths lived during the Ice Age.

mineral: A crystalline substance of regular atomic arrangement found in the earth. Rocks are made of two or more minerals.

paleontologist (pay-lee-ahn-TAH-luh-jist)**:** A scientist who studies prehistoric animal and plant life. The paleontologist examined the fossil for clues about the animal.

sedimentary rock: Rock formed from sediment (particles of sand, soil, and mud). Many fossils of dinosaurs were found deep within the sedimentary rock.

trilobite (TRIY-luh-biyt)**:** An extinct species of arthropod with three humps on each segment of its body. A trilobite fossil from the Paleozoic era found in the Burgess Shale gave paleontologists clues about the past.

LEARN

Activity 1: Let's Read! *(Online)*

Sometimes the most ordinary, familiar places have wonderful secrets. Sometimes they hold evidence of plants and animals that died out during Earth's ancient past. This evidence comes in the form of fossils.

Activity 2: Layering *(Offline)*

We can find fossils in many places—in rock formations, under ice, and even at the bottom of a lake. Experiment to discover how the layering of sediment at the bottoms of lakes creates fossils over time.

ASSESS

Lesson Assessment: Fossils and How They Form *(Online)*

You will complete an online assessment covering the main objectives of this lesson. Your assessment will be scored by the computer.

Name _____   Date _____

Fossils and How They Form
Layering
Follow the directions for the experiment, then answer the questions.

1. Pour 125mL (½ cup) of the white beans into a bowl.

2. Pour 125mL (½ cup) of the red beans into a second bowl.

3. Pour 125mL (½ cup) of the black beans into a third bowl.

4. Add ½ cup (125mL) of soil or sand to each bowl of beans.

5. Mix the beans and soil (or beans and sand) in each separate bowl.

6. Fill the baking dish halfway with water.

7. Slowly sprinkle the beans and soil (or beans and sand) mixture from one of the bowls into the water.

8. Wait 10 minutes and observe the layer.

9. Sprinkle the beans and soil (or beans and sand) mixture from another bowl into the water.

10. Wait 10 minutes and observe the layers now.

11. Add the last beans and soil (or beans and sand) mixture.

12. After 10 minutes, observe all three layers.

Draw the results after the final bowl of beans is added and 10 minutes have passed.

What happened to the soil or sand that was added with each bean layer?

_____

Consider each layer of beans a new layer of earth. Which color beans represent the oldest layer of earth?

_____

Why?

_____

Which bean layer represents the youngest layer?

_____

Why?

_____

Student Guide
Reading the Fossil Record

There are many types of fossils—petrified wood, cast, and mold fossils. Each fossile helps paleontologists unearth clues about the Earth's past and the organisms that lived during that time.

Lesson Objectives

- Explain that fossils help scientists reconstruct the history of life on Earth.
- Identify the different types of fossils, such as petrified, cast, and mold.
- State that fossils provide evidence that many kinds of organisms that once lived on Earth are now extinct.

PREPARE

Approximate lesson time is 60 minutes.

Advance Preparation

- If you don't already have it, you will need plaster of paris for the Make Your Own Fossil activity.

Materials

For the Student

> *Come Learn with Me: The Fossil Record and the History of Life* by Bridget Anderson
> Make a Fossil
> clay
> household item - paper cup
> household item - petroleum jelly
> household item - rolling pin
> household item - wax paper
> plaster of paris
> seashell
> graduated cylinder
> spoon - plastic
> timer

Keywords and Pronunciation

amber: A hard, often yellowish substance formed from fossilized tree sap. The insect was fossilized in the hardened amber.

cast fossil: A fossil formed when minerals replace animal tissue. A cast fossil is a three-dimensional view of the fossil remains.

decompose: To rot or decay. A dead animal's body will decompose over time.

decomposition: The process by which organic materials decay. Decomposition helps break down dead plants and animals.

mineralization: The process by which minerals replace the tissues of a dead organism. During mineralization, the skeleton of a dead animal hardens into rock.

paleontologist (pay-lee-ahn-TAH-luh-jist): A scientist who studies prehistoric animal and plant life. The paleontologist examined the fossil for clues about the animal.

sedimentary: Rock formed from sediment (particles of sand, soil, and mud). Sedimentary rock is an important part of the fossilization process.

sedimentary rock: Rock formed from sediment (particles of sand, soil, and mud). Fossils are often found in sedimentary rock throughout the world.

LEARN

Activity 1: Let's Read! *(Online)*

In many ways, scientists are like detectives. This is especially true of paleontologists. Learn how they use methods from many of the sciences—chemistry, biology, geology—to investigate things that happened thousands of years ago.

Activity 2: Make Your Own Fossil *(Offline)*

Use some ordinary materials to create cast and mold fossils.

ASSESS

Lesson Assessment: Reading the Fossil Record *(Online)*

You will complete an online assessment covering the main objectives of this lesson. Your assessment will be scored by the computer.

LEARN

Activity 3: Optional: Paleontologists *(Online)*

Are there many scientists who choose to become paleontologists? Are there female paleontologists?

You will be doing a web search to learn more. Web searches should always be done with adult supervision. K12 recommends the use of the safe search options that most web browsers come with, or one of the safe search engines produced by many major search engine providers.

Find more about this topic. Search for these key terms:

- paleontology
- paleontologists

Safety

As always, you may want to preview any recommended sites before your student views them.

Name _____ Date _____

Reading the Fossil Record
Make a Fossil

Follow the directions to make a seashell cast, then answer the question below.

1. Using a rolling pin, roll a piece of clay onto a piece of wax paper. You may choose the color. The flattened piece of clay should be about 3cm high and 5cm wide.

2. Coat the seashell with petroleum jelly and press it into the clay. Carefully remove the seashell. Wipe the excess petroleum jelly from the clay.

3. Observe the imprint the shell made. You now have a mold of the seashell.

4. Use more clay to build a wall about 1cm high around the edge of the flattened piece of clay. Secure the clay wall to the flattened piece so there are no holes under the wall. You will need the wall to hold in the plaster of Paris, which is like a thick liquid.

5. Place 70mL of the plaster of Paris into the paper cup. Slowly add about 25mL of water while mixing with the plastic spoon. The mixture should be thick but able to be poured. Add more water if necessary.

6. Fill the seashell imprint to the top of the wall with the plaster mixture.

7. Wait about 30 minutes for the plaster to dry. It should be hard when you place your finger on it.

8. Remove the clay surrounding the cast. Now you have a cast of the seashell.

What information can paleontologists learn from fossils?

_____

_____

_____

_____

_____

Student Guide

The Ever-Changing Earth

The Earth is constantly changing. Earthquakes shift the surface of the Earth as the oceans of the world change the shoreline of every landmass. How have the plants and animals of the Earth survived these changes? Explore the scientific theories about the changing world through geologic time.

Lesson Objectives

- Recognize that scientists think that many kinds of organisms once lived on Earth have completely disappeared.
- Recognize that scientists think that some organisms alive today resemble organisms of the distant past.
- State that geologic time is divided into four sections: Precambrian, Paleozoic, Mesozoic, and Cenozoic.
- Identify evidence from patterns in rock formations and fossils in rock layers to support possible explanations of Michigan's geological changes over time.

PREPARE

Approximate lesson time is 60 minutes.

Materials

For the Student

> *Come Learn with Me: The Fossil Record and the History of Life* by Bridget Anderson
> Solving the Riddles of Fossils

Keywords and Pronunciation

Cenozoic (see-nuh-ZOH-ihk)

continent: A great landmass on the surface of the Earth. The United States is located on the continent of North America.

Equus: The genus name scientists give to the group of animals that include modern horses. *Equus* is the only close relative of the Hyracotherium that lives today.

evolution: The gradual change of organisms over time. Through the process of evolution, species become well adapted to life on Earth.

extinct: No longer existing. If a type of organism is extinct, it has died out.

Hyracotherium: An early ancestor of the modern horse. *Hyracotherium* was a kind of small, dog-like animal that ate mostly fruits and plants.

Mesozoic (meh-zuh-ZOH-ihk)

Paleozoic (pay-lee-uh-ZOH-ihk)

Pangaea (pan-JEE-uh)**:** the name scientists give to a supercontinent that once existed on earth

Precambrian (pree-KAM-bree-uhn)

species (SPEE-sheez)**:** A group of organisms that share many characteristics and that can interbreed. Scientists think that species slowly changed throughout history as conditions changed on Earth.

LEARN

Activity 1: Let's Read *(Online)*

Our Earth has changed radically throughout history. Temperatures, scenery, and living creatures have changed a lot over time. The four main sections of what we call *geologic time* had very, very different living conditions. You may be surprised at what the evidence shows.

Activity 2: Rock Patterns and Fossils (Online)

Read through the activity to learn about how rocks and fossils can give clues about the geological changes Michigan has undergone over time.

Activity 3: Solving the Riddles of Fossils *(Offline)*

Paleontologists solve riddles all the time. They find scraps of evidence—scraps that are sometimes very tiny—and try to figure out what the evidence represents. Solve some fossil riddles yourself by reading clues and interpreting them.

ASSESS

Lesson Assessment: The Ever-Changing Earth *(Online)*

You will complete an online assessment covering the main objectives of this lesson. Your assessment will be scored by the computer.

Name _____   Date _____

The Ever-Changing Earth
Solving the Riddles of Fossils

Read each riddle, then solve it. (Hint: You'll find help in your text.)

1. I am a fossil of a fern that grew in the tropics. I was found in Antarctica, which is extremely cold. No one moved me, so why was I found in Antarctica?

   _____

2. I am a fossil of a coral that lived in the ocean. I was found on dry land, far from any ocean. If no one moved me, why would I be found in the middle of a continent?

   _____

   _____

3. I am a horse, but my ancestors didn't look anything like me. I'm much bigger than they are, and my teeth are a lot stronger. Why don't I look like earlier horses?

   _____

   _____

   _____

4. I am a fossil of an animal. A fossil of another animal was found in a younger layer of rock above me. He looks more like animals who are alive today than I do. Am I probably older or younger than the other fossil?

   _____

SUPER CHALLENGE: Name this era!

1. I am called the Age of Dinosaurs. _____

2. My name means *ancient life*, though sometimes I'm called the Age of Trilobites. _____

3. I am the era in which you live. _____

4. I am the longest period of geologic time. _____

Student Guide

The Precambrian Time and Paleozoic Era

What was the Precambrian time and Paleozoic era like? What organisms lived then? What major events define the eras? Search into the past and uncover the worlds of the Precambrian time and Paleozoic era.

Lesson Objectives

- Name one major event that occurred during the Paleozoic era.
- Name one major event that occurred during the Precambrian time.
- Name one organism that lived on the Earth during the Paleozoic era.
- Name one organism that lived on the Earth during the Precambrian time.

PREPARE

Approximate lesson time is 60 minutes.

Materials

For the Student

> *Come Learn with Me: The Fossil Record and the History of Life* by Bridget Anderson
> What Did the Moon See?

Keywords and Pronunciation

amphibian (am-FIH-bee-uhn)**:** A vertebrate that spends part of its life in water and part of its life on land. Frogs, toads, and salamanders are amphibians.

brachiopod (BRAY-kee-uh-pahd)

cyanobacteria (siy-A-nuh-bak-TIHR-ee-uh)**:** Bacteria that were one of the first forms of life on Earth. The earliest known fossils are of cyanobacteria.

meteorite (MEE-tee-uh-riyt)**:** A rocky object in space that falls to Earth before it burns up. A meteorite that hit the Earth made a crater as large as a football field.

Paleozoic (pay-lee-uh-ZOH-ihk)

Pangaea (pan-JEE-uh)**:** the name scientists give to a supercontinent that once existed on earth

Precambrian (pree-KAM-bree-uhn)

sedimentary rock: Rock formed from sediment (particles of sand, soil, and mud). Fossils are often found in sedimentary rock throughout the world.

stromatolite: A large colony of cynabacteria that grows like a reef of coral. Colonies of cyanobacteria form stromatolites that look like stone pillars in the ocean.

stromatolites (stroh-MA-tl-iyts)

trilobite (TRIY-luh-biyt)**:** An extinct species of arthropod with three humps on each segment of its body. A trilobite fossil from the Paleozoic era found in the Burgess Shale gave paleontologists clues about the past.

LEARN

Activity 1: Let's Read! *(Online)*

Volcanoes, earthquakes, and crashing meteorites were all part of the Earth's early years. A long time passed before life came about. Lean about the Precambrian time and Paleozoic era in Earth's history.

Activity 2: Diary of the Past *(Offline)*

If you could have been a witness to Earth's earliest years, what would you have seen? What would be your most important memories?

ASSESS

Lesson Assessment: The Precambrian Time and Paleozoic Era *(Online)*

You will complete an online assessment covering the main objectives of this lesson. Your assessment will be scored by the computer.

Name _____   Date _____

The Precambrian Time and Paleozoic Era
What Did the Moon See?

Imagine that you are the moon, looking down on the Earth. What would you have observed during the first two eras? Write your memories in this diary. The first entry has been written for you. Use the word bank below as you fill in the rest of your diary.

WORD BANK

stromatolites	worms	extinction
trilobites	ferns	brachiopod
plankton	Pangaea	mudflows
armor	climate changes	sponge
canyon	salty seas	

Beginning of time:

It's too dark to see much. There are a lot of meteorites, though, and they bang pretty hard. That poor planet is getting a lot of craters. There doesn't seem to be any life yet, but I'm optimistic. At this point there isn't even any oxygen, but I've already seen a lot of changes. At least the Earth is solid now—at first there was only a ball of gas.

Precambrian:

_____

_____

_____

_____

_____

_____

_____

_____

_____

_____

Paleozoic Era:

_____

_____

_____

_____

_____

_____

_____

_____

Student Guide

The Mesozoic and Cenozoic Eras

What were the Mesozoic and Cenozoic eras like? What organisms lived then? What major events define the eras? Search into the past and uncover the worlds of the Mesozoic and Cenozoic eras.

Lesson Objectives

- Name one major event that occurred during the Cenozoic era.
- Name one major event that occurred during the Mesozoic era.
- Name one major event that occurred in each of the four geologic sections: Precambrian, Paleozoic, Mesozoic, and Cenozoic.
- Name one organism that lived on the Earth during the Mesozoic era.

PREPARE

Approximate lesson time is 60 minutes.

Materials

For the Student

> *Come Learn with Me: The Fossil Record and the History of Life* by Bridget Anderson
> When Did It Happen?

Keywords and Pronunciation

asphalt: A black, tar-like substance. Asphalt fills The La Brea tar pits. Animals throughout the Cenozoic era became trapped in the tar.

Cenozoic (see-nuh-ZOH-ihk)

dinosaur: Any animal belonging to a group of large reptiles that lived in the Mesozoic era. Scientists think modern birds are descendants of Mesozoic dinosaurs.

ichthyosaur: An extinct marine reptile that lived in the Mesozoic era. Icthyosaurus had a dolphin-shaped body and a narrow, tooth-filled 'beak."

ichthyosaurus (ik-thee-uh-SAWR-uhs)

La Brea (luh BRAY-uh)

Mesozoic (meh-zuh-ZOH-ihk)

mosasaur (MOH-zuh-sawr): An extinct marine reptile that lived in the Mesozoic era. Mosasaur had a long head, a large jaw, a strong and flexible neck, and two strong pairs of paddles.

oviraptor (oh-vih-RAP-tur): A small, bird-like dinosaur that moved quickly on its two long legs. Oviraptor had a long tail, a curved neck, powerful jaws, and a strong beak.

plesiosaur (PLEE-see-uh-sawr): An extinct marine reptile that lived in the Mesozoic era. Mary Anning, a female fossil collector, found the first plesiosaur fossil.

---

protoceratops (proh-toh-SEHR-uh-tahps)

pterosaur (TEHR-uh-sawr)

velociraptor (vuh-LAH-suh-rap-tuhr)**:** An extinct reptile that lived in the Mesozoic era. The velociraptor was a particularly vicious dinosaur.

LEARN

Activity 1: Let's Read! *(Online)*

How did the Earth look when dinosaurs were alive? How did it look when there was only one continent? Read pages 36 to 45 to learn about the evidence scientists have found.

Activity 2: When Did It Happen? *(Offline)*

The Mesozoic and Cenozoic Eras were very different. Using your book, tell which events and which organisms belong to each period.

ASSESS

Lesson Assessment: The Mesozoic and Cenozoic Eras *(Online)*

You will complete an online assessment covering the main objectives of this lesson. Your assessment will be scored by the computer.

Name _____   Date _____

The Mesozoic and Cenozoic Eras

When Did It Happen?

Some of these events happened in the Mesozoic Era, while others happened in the Cenozoic Era. Write an M next to each description that fits the Mesozoic Era, and write a C next to each description that fits the Cenozoic Era.

1. Humans use fire for cooking. _____

2. Pangaea breaks apart. _____

3. Land animals begin to have live babies instead of laying eggs. _____

4. Continents move toward their current locations. _____

5. Dinosaurs live and roam the Earth. _____

6. Animals get stuck in LaBrea Tar Pits. _____

7. Temperature drops worldwide. _____

8. Plesiosaurs and oviraptors live. _____

9. Ice forms at north and south poles. _____

10. The first large forests and open woodlands develop. _____

11. Early humans make tools. _____

12. A mass extinction occurs. _____

For each of these sets of events, scientific evidence suggests which happened first, second, and last. Put the events in order by writing 1, 2, or 3 in the spaces provided.

13.

   A. Dinosaurs come into being. _____

   B. Birds come into being. _____

   C. Animals similar to crocodiles learn to run on their hind legs. _____

14.

   A. Humans settle down to live in communities. _____

   B. Organisms adapt to colder environments. _____

   C. Sea levels drop, exposing more land. _____

Student Guide

Fossils and Geologic Time: Unit Review and Assessment

What have you learned about fossils and geologic time? Play a game and review what you have learned about the earliest parts of Earth's history!

Lesson Objectives

- Describe the conditions under which fossils may form and distinguish among the different types, such as petrified, mold, and cast.
- Explain that fossils provide information about organisms that lived long ago and help scientists reconstruct the history of life on Earth.
- Name one major event that occurred in each of the four geologic sections: Precambrian, Paleozoic, Mesozoic, and Cenozoic.
- Recognize that scientists divide geologic time into four main sections (Precambrian, Paleozoic, Mesozoic, and Cenozoic) and that each section covers one major stage in Earth's history.
- State that fossils provide evidence that many kinds of organisms that once lived on Earth are now extinct.

PREPARE

Approximate lesson time is 60 minutes.

Materials

For the Student

> Fossils and Geologic Time Review Cards
> *Come Learn with Me: The Fossil Record and the History of Life* by Bridget Anderson

LEARN

Activity 1: Review the Book *(Offline)*

How much do you remember about fossils and geologic time? Look back through the book to review the things you have learned about the different eras in Earth's early history.

Instructions

Take a moment to look back through the book. Look at the pictures. Can you explain what is shown in each? After you have looked at each picture, review the glossary for words you learned during the unit.

Now use your knowledge of fossils and geologic time to answer each clue on the cards. Write your answer below each question on the solid line at the bottom of the card. After you have answered all the questions, check your answers. Correct any errors you may have made.

Now play a game with the cards. Cut out the cards, then cut each card in half on the dotted line. Turn the cards face down and arrange them in a square of four rows and four columns.

Turn one card over and read it to yourself. Then turn another card over. Do they match? You are looking for a question and its answer. If they are not a match, turn them back over and repeat with two new cards. Pay close attention to where you place the cards—it may help you make a match!

The game is over when you have matched all the cards.

ASSESS

Unit Assessment: Fossils and Geologic Time (*Online*)

Complete an online Unit Assessment. The computer will score the assessment.

LEARN

Activity 2: Optional: ZlugQuest Measurement (*Online*)

Name _____   Date _____

Fossils and Geologic Time:
Unit Review and Assessment

Fossils and Geologic Time Review Cards

I am a supercontinent. I formed during the Paleozoic era and broke apart in the Mesozoic era. What am I?	I am a fossil. I am made of dead wood that has hardened into stone. What kind of fossil am I?
Answer: _____	Answer: _____
I am an era in geologic time. In this time, humans created tools and formed communities. Which era am I?	The Earth was just a ball of gases and hot lava when I began. Later, cyanobacteria filled the water. Which period of geological time am I?
Answer: _____	Answer: _____
When a rock hardens inside a mold fossil, I am formed. What kind of fossil am I?	Velociraptors, proceratopses, and other dinosaurs roamed the Earth during my time period. Which era am I?
Answer: _____	Answer: _____

I hold an imprint of the shape and texture of something ancient. I may have been mud that has hardened into stone. What kind of fossil am I?	I provide evidence of organisms that are now extinct. By studying me, scientists can reconstruct the history of the Earth. What am I?
Answer: _____	Answer: _____